1st 7hus

fene/fone

Folklore and Society

Series Editors
Roger Abrahams
Bruce Jackson
Marta Weigle

A list of books in the series appears at the end of this book.

Publications of the American Folklore Society

NEW SERIES

General Editor, Patrick B. Mullen

The Lost World of the Craft Printer

THE LOST WORLD OF THE
Craft Printer

Maggie Holtzberg-Call

UNIVERSITY OF ILLINOIS PRESS
Urbana and Chicago

Publication of this book was made possible in part by the generosity of
The Carl and Lily Pforzheimer Foundation, Inc.

This book is printed on acid-free paper.

Library of Congress Cataloging-in-Publication Data

Holtzberg-Call, Maggie, 1955-
   The lost world of the craft printer / Maggie Holtzberg-Call.
     p. cm. —(Folklore and society) (Publication of the
American Folklore Society. New series)
   Includes bibliographical references and index.
   ISBN 0–252–01799–4 (cloth: acid-free paper)
   1. Printing industry—Social aspects—United States. 2. Printers—
United States—Folklore. 3. Printing—United States—History.
4. Folklore—United States. I. Title. II. Series. III. Series:
Publications of the American Folklore Society. New series
(Unnumbered)
Z243.U5H67 1992
338.8′2616862′0973—dc20   90–24004
                                         CIP

To the memory of my brother, David

Then let us sing as we nimbly fling
The slender letters round;
A glorious thing is our laboring,
Oh where can the like be found.

from "The Printer's Song," *Voice of Industry,* 1845

It was a romantic trade. You did things with your hands.
It was creative. . . . Now it's not like that anymore, you
know. Everything is cut and dried on the machine.

—Fil Valdez, compositor

Contents

Illustrations

Preface

An eighty-one-year-old retired printer once told me that when *he* was young, printers wore high hats. "Today," he complained, "it's nothing. It's all machine stuff." A more recent retiree put it bluntly. "Frankly, let's settle the whole thing now: There are no more printers. It goes right from the editorial room to the press, eliminating the composing room entirely."

I would not have to go far to hear the same story, many times over, from printers occupationally displaced by technological change. It is a story told with rhetoric glorifying the old days of "harder work," "cruder conditions," "better quality," and "more highly developed skills."

Though the subjects of this book are craftspeople in the printing trade, their words and collective perspective address a crucial aspect of modern American life, for occupational displacement affects millions. Whether one is listening to older printers, machinists, carpenters, railroad workers, cowboys, or commercial fishermen, the old ways come out sounding better—at least for people, past their prime, looking back and reflecting on the juxtaposition between the past and the present world.

By focusing on the rhetoric of craftspeople displaced from the printing trade, I hope to communicate something of the narrative structure and function of occupational nostalgia, while celebrating the triumph of people who, connected through their work identities, have adapted to the deskilling of craft labor and the threat of unemployment. In a time characterized by a growing population of technological retirees, the printers' adaptation will certainly resonate with the increasing numbers of workers whose traditional craft skills are being similarly undermined by technological innovations.

When I speak of hot-metal printers, I am referring to the work of compositors, stonehands, and Linotype operators engaged in the physical production of printed words. Theirs was an occupation with a five-hundred-year history, shaped by trade identification and tradition. Printing was considered a prestigious trade and printers dressed accordingly. A compositor who spent more than fifty working years on Chicago's Printers Row reminisces: "To someone who had finished only one year of high school, a 'compositor' had the connotation of status and of dignity. We came to work dressed with tie and collar . . . a man came by every week to sell us clean aprons, as well as sand soap to remove the printers' ink."[1]

As wordsmiths, the printers' command of language made them unique among labor craftspeople. Barnie Weeks, president of the Alabama Labor Council for twenty-seven years, describes printers in the 1930s, during his apprenticeship:

"Printers not only were by and large all high school graduates, they constantly read. They had to set the stories up in print. And the proofreaders of course had to really assimilate what they were reading; they had to be sure of the sentence structure and everything else. You learned punctuation. You learned spelling. You learned sentence structure. And before long you found that you liked to read, so you were reading when you were *not* at work, as well as when you were at work."[2]

Membership in an intellectual craft was a point of pride. Earl Powell, a working printer in his late seventies, said, "To me, printing is the most important business that the world's ever known because without printing we would have no religion, we'd have no law, we'd have no medicine . . . 90 percent of all of our knowledge was gained through the printed word."[3]

Powell's spoken sentiment is paralleled in print by men of

letters. Sigfrid H. Steinberg: "Neither political, constitutional, ecclesiastical, and economic events, nor sociological, philosophical, and literary movements can be fully understood without taking into account the influence which the printing press has exerted upon them."[4] Francis Bacon: "We should note the force, effect, and consequences of inventions which are nowhere more conspicuous than in those three which were unknown to the ancients, namely, printing, gunpowder, and the compass. For these three have changed the appearance and state of the whole world."[5]

Hot-metal printers identify with famous names in American letters—they customarily point with pride to writers who began as printer's apprentices: Benjamin Franklin, Horace Greeley, Mark Twain, Walt Whitman, Edgar Allan Poe, Joel Chandler Harris, Sherwood Anderson, and Erskine Caldwell, to name a few. But the trade of printing, as they, and many generations before them, knew it, is no longer practiced at large.

During the late 1960s and early 1970s the handicraft technology of wood and molten lead, known as hot metal, met its demise. Computer-aided typesetting and offset printing have taken its place. In the transition, the hot-metal printer has had to cope with displacement, planned attrition, early retirement, the deskilling of craft labor, and the loss of occupational status. No more high hats. The legacy of an elevated status makes their fall that much greater.[6]

What follows is based, in large part, on the spoken words of craftspeople whose training and skills were shaped in a world of trade-specific traditions, tools, techniques, and terminology. Unexpectedly, the world changed and the workers were bumped off their collective career trajectories. Derailment motivated some to adapt, others to deny; for most it has also engendered a need to make sense of lost status and the downgrading of their craft. Printers manifest this need by giving voice to their occupational nostalgia through a rhetoric of displacement. For them, the rhetoric is a way to construct self-images worth living with. For me, the rhetoric is a way into a world worth knowing.

Notes

1. Mike Franklin, "An Ethereal Long Weekend," *The Printer* (July 1990): 8.

2. Tape-recorded interview with Barnie Weeks at the Alabama State Council on the Arts, Montgomery, Alabama, 12 December 1988. Weeks served a five-year apprenticeship on a Montgomery weekly newspaper in the early 1930s. After working with the *Advertiser Journal* for twenty-one years, he was elected president of the Alabama Labor Council (the AFL-CIO encompassing all unions of Alabama) and served until his retirement in 1983.

3. Earl Powell, tape-recorded conversation at Heritage Printers, Charlotte, North Carolina, 13 November 1986.

4. Sigfrid H. Steinberg, *Five Hundred Years of Printing*, 3d ed. (London: Penguin Books, 1974), 17.

5. Quoted in Elizabeth Eisenstein's *The Printing Press as an Agent of Change* (Cambridge: Cambridge University Press, 1979), 43.

6. The printers' elevated social status dates back to the Middle Ages, when craft guilds were numerous. Printers were the only craftsmen allowed to carry a sword while moving about. Carl Schlesinger, personal communication, February 1990.

Acknowledgments

I am grateful above all others to the printers who shared with me their knowledge and love of the trade. I thank them for their participation in and enthusiasm for my efforts to document their words and ways.

There are those I wish to acknowledge in connection with seeing this book through completion, and perhaps more important, in inspiring the vague notion of its beginnings. It was Special Collections Librarian Elizabeth A. Swaim and bibliophile friends Sue and Greer Allen who first introduced me to the world of fine typography. Stimulating talks with Mark Simos on the nexus between language, computers, and the folklore of printing encouraged me to pursue this research and led me to some valuable informants.

Three academic teachers stand out for their inspirational courses and writings, and for the ideas and dialogue generated in our office hour talks. Henry Glassie brought the discipline of folklore to life, demonstrating its potential as a humanistic endeavor. Ray L. Birdwhistell taught me the importance of locating one's perspective, and of finding the right questions. His teachings will stay with me for a long time to come. And Kenneth S. Goldstein, a former printer himself, shared his experiences of the trade and of the trade's relevance to folklore.

I owe special gratitude to Archie Green—folklorist, advocate, labor historian, trade unionist, and former shipwright—who has come to be a valued friend. We have corresponded through several drafts of this work. It was Archie who suggested key bibliography, who supplied me with a steady stream of printing-lore ephemera, who stressed the importance of including examples from the world of fiction, the visual arts, and popular culture, and who guided the progress of this book with the spirit of a coach encouraging his trainee.

In addition, I must mention Carl Schlesinger who, having read the manuscript, generously shared his encyclopedic knowledge of the printing trade, as well as his personal insight into the toll that technological changes have wrought on working printers. He provided technical and anecdotal information, correcting subtleties of language with the confidence of a native speaker.

Closer to home are my parents. Their love, support, and genuine interest engendered confidence and provided opportunity.

Finally, I wish to thank Malcolm Call, who believed in what I was doing. He has been generous and supportive throughout the writing process, always willing to lend his full attention and editorial eye. His companionship, and his passion for making books and for taking risks, kept me going.

The Lost World of the Craft Printer

1

Introduction

"I've been to wakes where they couldn't get the ink off the corpse's fingers," Ed Jacob said. The confession set Ed apart, even though he and Dick Harrison shared the experience of being printers who successfully made the transition from "hot type," which relied on the manual operation of Linotype machines, to "cold type," in which computer keyboarding generates type in photoprocessors. When I first met them, they were both employed at a downtown Philadelphia computer typesetting house; it was midday and busy in the company cafeteria.

In reply to my question of how he had entered the trade, Dick Harrison recounted his career to date—high school shop teacher, journeyman proofreader, a degree in printing management, and his current position as manager of computer systems. His answer finished, he turned the attention to Ed. Rather than offer his own equivalent of Dick's curriculum vitae, Ed gave us a glimpse into a world where deceased printers were buried with ink under their fingernails.

Not everyone takes his or her trade so visibly to the grave. The message behind the drama seemed to be about fellowship. Being a printer was not necessarily *what* you had done, but *who* you had done it with. Ed had come by the printer's trade in a traditional way, that is, a six-year apprenticeship in the composing room of a top-quality publisher. His talk revealed a lifetime spent around old-time printers.

"I *am* a dying breed. There's not many of us left. In fact, that's what was brought up at the GPO [Government Printing

Office] last week. This fella, he's close to my age, he said, 'Boy, there's so few of us left.'

"You know," Ed said as if realizing it for the first time, "I've seen a craft disappear in my lifetime." [1]

A similar work history motivated former Linotype operator Bob Culp to encourage me to speak with a retired coworker of his before it was too late. "He was a *printer.*" Bob paused on the word "printer" as if a fermata[2] hovered above it, and then he asked, "Do you know what I mean when I say that?" After seven years of questioning, reading, listening, and observing, I think I do.

This book is an attempt to convey that understanding, to describe not only the customs, the tools, the terminology, and the values, but what tied them all together to make meaning for those who were printers. The meaning is stored in their collective occupational experience, and it is what motivates them to traditionalize the present and reconstruct the past in patterned ways. An example of such patterned communication is the rhetoric of tradition which pervades printers' occupational narratives.

"Rhetoric of tradition"? A craft that knows it is dying, with little chance of revitalization, develops a tradition of tradition. Much like historical periodization, worlds are delineated and temporally juxtaposed. A generation of individuals with comparable occupational experience marks and assigns meaning to this shared "world" of the past replete with language, techniques, tools, materials, and standards of workmanship.

Though they do not have a name for it, printers do have clearly established ways of talking about their occupational past. In persuasive and at times poetic speech, printers convey the relevance of tradition to the printing trade today. Reconstructive narratives about work processes in a different time with a different technology express attitudes about craft excellence, quality, and technological change—attitudes that are conditioned by the printers' hot-metal experience.

A reductionist who considers these narratives might be satisfied by concluding that people with similar experiences tell similar stories, and leave it at that. It is the simple truth of such a statement that I, as a folklorist, find compelling. One might assume that the patterns and themes that emerge in these stories are "the result of individual perceptions of objectively similar events,"[3] but such a view overlooks the social and communicative aspects of *processing* experience. Experience alone does not generate genre-specific narratives, *people* do—people acting in relation to other people to maintain a degree of social connectedness.

People tell similar stories in part because they have learned to. Any study that attempts to deal with a group's oral testimony must take into account the making of group identity, whether it is an identity based upon occupation, ethnicity, social class, or artistry. Membership, and the sense of belonging it engenders, comes not only from sharing life experiences, but also from communicating anticipated experience and retrospective experience. One must have personalized stories to fill generic slots—stories of initiation rituals, of apprenticeships, of botched jobs, of superb workmanship—in order to claim membership.

The similarity in patterns and themes that emerge in narrators' accounts is due to the shared cultural experience that teaches us what to remember and what to forget, what is worth recounting, when, where, how, and with whom. It is in this sense that any narrative about a printer, told by a printer, is essential to *being* a printer.

Technological development shapes and reshapes the narrative environment peculiar to the printing trade. Changes in technology affect work processes, attitudes toward work, and occupational language. The two major technological innovations to hit the typesetter's post-Gutenberg world could be said to be the introduction of mechanical typesetting, or "hot metal," in the late 1880s and the advent of computer-aided photocomposition, or "cold type," which began in the late 1940s and continues to this day with advances in laser technology.

The electronics boom of the 1950s was in large part responsible for the transition from hot metal to cold composition.[4] The shift reflects an ongoing technological change in our society characterized by a move away from visible forces (mechanically moving parts) toward invisible forces (electronics, optics, and computer digitization). At some level, what printers have experienced, auto builders, papermill workers, carpenters, diamond cutters, dressmakers, and railroad engineers have also experienced. As a microcosm of technological change and the culture of change, the printers' experience provides a useful case study for exploring nostalgia and the rhetoric of tradition.

A study of this kind of occupational folklore is needed because all of our occupations are undergoing a similar transformation. We are in transition from an industrial to an information economy where work is increasingly carried out in computer-mediated environments. The age of the smart machine[5] is upon us. "Accomplishing work [comes] to depend more upon thinking about and responding to an electronically presented symbolic medium than upon acting out know-how derived from sentient experience."[6]

In a sense, we are witnessing the death of "stuff" in material form. Type is no longer "live" or "dead" as it was once called by the hot-metal compositor, but exists as electrical impulses in the metaphysical space of computer memory. The printer's use of language gives us the human side of technological retooling. More important, it gives us insight into one of the ways in which people maintain a sense of meaningful continuity in the face of transformational change.

The Printer: A Definition

Like any generic term, the word "printer" can be cause for confusion since it is commonly used to refer to a number of people employed in the allied printing trades, including compositors (typesetting and page makeup), lithographers, photoengravers, and press operators. The titles of "printer," "typographer," "typesetter," "compositor," and "pressman" have meant different things in different times. In the late 1970s, A. H. Raskin observed that "the typographical union bargains for the employees called printers—who, as it happens, do no printing."[7]

In Joseph Moxon's day, there was enough discrepancy for him to try and set the record straight in his *Mechanick Exercises on the Whole Art of Printing (1683–4)*, reputed to be the earliest manual of printing. His detailed text, describing tools and skilled movements, put in writing what had existed, up until that time, wholly as privileged and ephemeral knowledge circulating in oral tradition.[8]

Moxon differentiates between printers and typographers, ranking the latter higher in their command of the mathematical sciences and requisite knowledge of all three trades: typefounding, punchcutting, and printing. In the late seventeenth century, the typographers' trade was all-encompassing; a typographer had mastered the work of the compositor, the corrector, the "press-man," and "the inck-maker" [*sic*]. For Moxon, printing was to typography as carpentry was to architecture: "By a typographer I do *not* [my emphasis] mean a printer, . . . any more than Dr. Dee means a carpenter or mason to be an architect: But by a typographer I mean such a one who by his own judgement can either perform or direct others to perform from the beginning to the end, all the handy-works and physical operations related to Typographie."[9]

And yet the Oxford English Dictionary entry for *typographer,* under which Moxon's statement appears, reads, "One who is skilled in typography; a printer,"[10] as if the two words were interchangeable. Even today the imprecision persists; "printer" can refer to the workman employed at the press, the business itself, or the whirring, clacking machinery used for printing. The term may mean the large commercial printing plant which handles everything from typesetting copy to binding books, the "Speedy Print" job printer, or the latest in home computer equipment.

The mutational character of the word "printer" stems from changes in technological processes and the gradual move toward specialization. At one time, the craft of printing and the enterprise of editing and publishing were productively integrated under one roof (as it is once again with desktop publishing). During the mid-nineteenth century, when capital became indispensable in the establishment of a successful printing shop, the business of publishing and editing separated from the craft of printing. The average journeyman printer could no longer aspire to become a master printer who edited and published his own work.[11]

In the late nineteenth and early twentieth centuries, a significant portion of the journeyman printer's work was subject to mechanization and the division of labor into more specialized tasks. This translated into a decrease in the overall knowledge, training, and skill required of individual craftspeople. That is, a printer was even less likely to become competent in Moxon's full range of "handy-works and physical operations" related to typography.

It was in 1857 that the National Typographical Union (which would become the International Typographical Union [ITU] in 1869) adopted a resolution recognizing two classes only in the typographical profession: compositors and pressmen.[12] This official acknowledgment of the trade's separate branches did not address the all-inclusive nature of the class "printer," which continues to fall prey to claims of exclusivity. The title is not readily shared. Bertram Powers, longtime president of the New York City local of the International Typographical Union, made the following comment, attesting to the competitive monopoly over the title: "*Printer means composing.* The compositors think *they're* the printers 'cause they set the type, and the pressmen think *they're* the printers 'cause they print the ink. With the merging of the allied printing trades, the problem will be solved."[13]

Sandy Bevis, a former president of the International Typographical Union, worked his way around to a similar conclusion:

"At one time, the printer was generic and if you asked anybody who was associated with the industry what they did, they were a printer. Presswork was printing, very definitely. Making up pages in a commercial plant or newspaper was printing. Bindery work was printing in a sense because it was handling of printing. . . . Generically, I think these people would consider themselves printers.

"When they pinned them down to what they did, they'd say, 'Well, I'm in the bindery department,' or 'I'm in the pressroom.'

It got so the printers were more or less considered to be in the composing room, by the other crafts." [14]

Tensions between compositors and pressmen were felt as early as 1874 when pressmen made efforts to charter their own union, against the wishes of the ITU. In twenty years' time, the International Printing Pressmen Union, the International Typographical Union, and the International Brotherhood of Bookbinding each recognized the others' jurisdiction. The Allied Printing Trade Association was formed in 1910. In the 1980s it became clear that technology had obliterated many of the jurisdictional lines that once separated stereotypers from photoengravers, and compositors from pressmen.

As printing technology continues to evolve, so will definitions of the tradespeople involved in bringing us the printed word. For practical purposes, a printer is defined here as a member of an occupational group whose craft involves the quality reproduction of written texts. My concern here is primarily with hot-metal compositors, those craftspeople who set type by hand or machine, correct composed type, and make up pages to prepare them for presswork.

The Folklorist's Lens

Training in folklore can give one a passion and respect for people's spoken words while providing a methodology for interpreting their meaning. The heart of this book is based on oral narratives elicited in qualitative, exploratory interviews with a core of helpful, opinionated, articulate people. Their statements have been a source of ongoing inspiration. As one folklore scholar put it, "No observer, neither psychiatrist nor poet, can draw out all the psyche of another. Our understanding of the mind . . . remains at an excruciatingly primitive level, but such hints as we do have require us to read people directly in their own statements in which the fullness of consciousness might be caught, rather than indirectly through someone else's clinical report or judgmental commentary." [15]

Fieldwork, in the anthropological sense, evokes intensive interaction with a given population over a substantial period of time, in a mappable locale. The "field" of my fieldwork, however, knows no geographic bounds; one finds displaced printers everywhere. Research has taken me from the historical centers of American printing and publishing—Philadelphia, Baltimore, and New York City—to the southern city of Charlotte, North Carolina, where I found one of the few extant printing establishments maintaining a commercially viable hot-metal operation. There I met people working with their hands, actively engaged in processes that others could speak of only in memories. Travel to the Union Printers Home in Colorado Springs was invaluable. Gathered in one place were retired and infirm printers from all over North America, eager to share recollections of their craft.

The lack of a geographically delimited "field" in this work has proved an asset, highlighting the vitality of a folk community based upon occupational identity. A generation of geographically dispersed printers is culturally connected; the similarity in their attitudes and the structural consistency in their narratives of common occupational experience tell us so.

The classic nineteenth-century definition of a folk group idealized the rural, unsophisticated, isolated agrarian community. Visions of Redfieldian peasants and Appalachian mountain folk untouched by modern civilization come to mind.[16] In the twentieth century, this definition expanded to include any group of people who share at least one factor in common (language, lore, custom, belief) and who have developed a sense of community. A folk group can be distinguished by region, ethnicity, occupation, age, or religion—that societal element which binds people together in face-to-face interaction.[17]

The endurance of the printers' verbal and material folklore, which transcends time and space, challenges traditional notions about the definition of folk groups and the very meaning of groupness, itself. Printers are an occupational group not bounded by space or time, yet they share an enduring group identity evidenced in words, in actions, and in the products of their labor. It is a fact that even printers separated by the waters of the Atlantic Ocean voice essentially the same sentiments in both form and content.[18] Certainly no one would think to put these two groups together in the traditional sense of group; they are individuals who have never and will never meet.

On another level, old-style printers typify occupational folklore at its most romantic. They are a dying breed in a dying craft, especially the people who worked in the composing department where foundry type was set up in forms, corrected, and made ready for presswork.

The "dying-art syndrome" is a familiar refrain in the history of folklore scholarship. There is nothing like the recognition of a soon-to-be-lost art or artifact to inspire collecting, documentation, and rhetoric. Older is better. Endangered is best. We perform a cultural service by collecting and preserving. As William McNeil notes in his study on the history of early American folklore scholarship, this justification for the recording of folklore had become a tradition in itself by the late nineteenth century.[19]

This get-it-before-it-goes attitude was shared by the people I interviewed, most notably among those who had made the transition from hot to cold type. After my initial conversation with Dick Harrison and Ed Jacob, employees at a computer typesetting firm, Dick said to me, "I think I know what you're trying to do. You're trying to do the *Foxfire* of typography. Ed and I came from the hot-metal days. We're glad you're interested."

Later, in the middle of a heated discussion on the effects of modern technology on the printing industry in America, Ed interrupted himself and said, "I'd like to see you do this because it won't be too long before it won't be available."

The "it" Ed referred to is the older generation of trade printers and the conventions of hot-metal typography to which they have traditionally adhered. Many of the long-standing rules and conventions of good printing practice are in fact the direct result of the built-in limitations of working in hot metal. As limitations are eliminated by technological innovation, so is the need for skills once required of the hot-metal compositor.

Consider the following: To make a "boxed rule" around a block of metal type, one has to mitre strips of lead rule, a process which leaves alloy shavings on the floor. With the changeover to photographic processes, one can use the graphic designer's roll of rule tape and simply superimpose the corner of one rule on another to form a box. Sawing, rearranging, and leading Linotype slugs of type involve very different skills from word processing via a computer keyboard.

With a major change in technology, conventions are more easily questioned and rules are more easily broken. Given this, it seems important, especially to older printers who apprenticed in hot-metal composing rooms, to remember those occupational skills, jargon, customs, techniques, values, and pride that were an integral part of the hot-metal handicraft tradition. Much of the meaning of the work seems to be located in the tangibility and intrinsic constraints of working in hot-metal methods. The latter process embodies qualities that one associates with craft: skill, patience, pride in workmanship, control. For these journeymen the process evokes all that is good about tradition. Hot metal is nearly coterminous with tradition, indeed craft excellence. As Ed Jacob put it, while speaking about early-twentieth-century printing, "Craftsmanship was common. It was the tradition then."

If we envision tradition as culturally assigned meaning,[20] we can then ask, what meaning has been assigned to hot metal by these people? Their occupational narratives resonate with clues. It is through textual analysis of such talk that we come to see how compositors traditionalize their experience. In other words, by studying such behavior we gain an understanding of how meaning is constructed, evoked, and communicated.

One of the problems inherent in interview-based research is assessing the impact of data-gathering on the data gathered. As with all discourse, context shapes the form and content of what is said and what is left unsaid. The interview, as a mode of communication in social science research, "encapsulates our own native theories of communication and reality." It is a socially accepted way of acquiring and conveying information, and its compatibility with other systems of acquiring and conveying information must be assessed.[21] The interview, transcribed and analyzed, is less of a reflection of what is "out there" and more an interpretation which is jointly created by the interviewer and the interviewee.

Ray Birdwhistell put this so well one day when he confessed, "I can't get it out of my head, that if I get agreement with an informant, I've got the truth. It's not the truth, it's merely collusion."

The texts that serve as primary source material in this study are, for the most part, interview-elicited narratives, which means, given communicative norms, I exercised the interviewer's overriding rights of asking the questions, introducing new topics, and controlling the overall shape of discourse. Given this inherent imbalance, I made special efforts to conduct open-ended exploratory interviews. The oral texts that people this book were spoken to me, and are therefore a product of our social communication. They are not necessarily representative of what these individuals might say among themselves; that I cannot know.

In the text and endnotes, I have tried to give a sense of my relationship with these speakers—how I came to know them, what my formal relationship to them was, whether coworker, interested student, or ethnographic researcher, and the degree of trust and friendship that developed between us. The variation in how these individuals are referred to in the text is intentional, an effort to reflect accurately the degree of formality, or lack of it, in our social interactions. That is, I felt the reader has a right to know that I was on a first-name basis with some people and not with others.

Nearly a decade ago, it was my discovery of the simple beauty of letterforms that initiated my journey into the printer's world. Working in the special collections of a university library, I was introduced to the world of fine typography and printing. Subsequent employment in university publishing and commercial typesetting provided me with hands-on experience in the printing trade. I have learned what it is to "spec" type,[22] price type, arrange type, and talk type. As either a client, a coworker, or an independent researcher, I have interacted with a broad range of individuals who affect and are affected by changes in the printing industry. Among these individuals are Linotype operators, stonehands, compositors, proofreaders, computer keyboarders, pasteup artists, printing-firm sales representatives and tour guides, book publishers (editors, designers, production managers), rare book librarians, typographical union presidents, printing equipment auctioneers, and a journeyman lettercutter.

In order to best utilize my time with such individuals it was necessary beforehand to delve into a variety of written sources which would provide historical context and a basic technical know-how of the printing trade. The literature on printing history, including such works as Steinberg's *Five Hundred Years of Printing,*[23] Moxon's manual, Tracy's history of the Typographical Union,[24] Seybold's *World of Digital Typesetting,*[25] and Moran's *Printing Presses,*[26] was useful in understanding the material side of technological change. A wealth of information exists in trade literature: union weeklies, advertisements, trade journals, printing dictionaries, type specimen books, and instruction manuals on the practice of printing. I have also engaged the literary companionship of "gentlemen typographers"—men and women such as William Morris, Eric Gill, Beatrice Warde, Frederic Goudy, Daniel B. Updike, and Carl P. Rollins—all of whose delightful little books practice what they preach.

For indices of more widespread cultural meanings of craft labor, it has been useful to examine portrayals of printers by literary artists (writers of short stories, novelists, poets) and visual artists (sculptors, painters, cartoonists, film producers). These creative works capture and comment on the atmosphere, working lives, technical skills, aspirations, language, and gestures of craftspeople in the printing trade.

For example, if we look back to the 1930s, it is clear that the American worker had become a symbol of the proletarian struggle for power. Artists turned their talents to depicting laborers as the dominant motif in their work, rather than a detail of background. Internationally renowned sculptor Max Kalish (1891–1945) cre-

Fig. 1. Max Kalish, *Compositor,* bronze. Photo by Paul Hexter.

ated numerous bronzes of laborers in action—farmers tossing pitchforks of hay, riveters welding steel beams, compositors making up pages, fishermen pulling in nets, ditchdiggers, barge toilers, glassblowers, rail-tie spikers, and foundrymen—because he wanted others to be aware of the beauty of laborers' movements and the importance of their place in American industrialized society. In Kalish's words: "We must learn to create from the living present. In this great industrial age, tremendous heroic tasks are being performed, and it is here that we will find our greatest art expression. As I mingle among the workers in factories or in the open, I find them in their natural poses. . . . In the performance of them there is strength and grace, while at rest there is a sense of rhythm and beauty that compares favorably with the greatest sculptural themes of the past."[27]

Kalish's *Compositor,* a large bronze figure of a newspaper compositor making up a page, found an appreciative audience in the lobby of a great metropolitan newspaper. Smaller bronze replicas of the piece, these entitled *The Make-Up Man,* were cast. Emblematic of the craftsman's trade, these bronze casts adorned the bookcases of printing establishments throughout the country.

David Smith (1906–65), a pivotal figure in modern American sculpture, chose to interpret the printer's art in his 1954 piece *Sitting Printer.* During the mid-1950s Smith experimented with the use of "found objects" from industrial detritus. In this case, the lifesize anthropomorphic torso is made from a cast of an empty compositor's case which continues to evoke associations with the object's earlier use.[28]

Frederic W. Goudy (1865–1947) was one of the most prolific type designers in printing history. Associated with such classic typefaces as Goudy Modern, Forum, and Kennerly, Goudy's name became familiar in print shops across the country. Frederic and his coworker wife, Bertha, are commemorated in a painting by Robert Thom. The type designer is portrayed refining the italic letter *Q* for his typeface Deepdene. Sketches for lowercase letters are shown tacked to the wall. Bertha is in the background, filling a composing stick with foundry type.[29]

Fig. 2. David Smith, *Sitting Printer,* bronze, 87¼ × 15¾ × 16 inches. Storm King Art Center, Mountainville, N.Y. Gift of the Ralph E. Ogden Foundation, 1967.9.

Fig. 3. Robert Thom, *Frederic and Bertha Goudy*. From the Kimberly-Clark collection, "Graphic Communications through the Ages," College of Graphic Arts and Photography, Rochester Institute of Technology, Rochester, N.Y. Photo by Robert Kushner. Used with permission.

This book began as a folkloric study using the oral testimony of living printers as a primary source, that is, the testimony of craftspeople whose union had essentially negotiated itself out of existence. By the mid-1980s, the trade as it had been known for centuries was virtually gone. Facing the futility of prolonging archaic work practices only to save jobs in the short run, union officials made the best settlement possible and managed to protect its membership through the demise.

Some printers were able to retrain and remain in the industry through the 1970s, even though manning computer-operated terminals and handling paper and paste bore little resemblance to printing as they knew it. Their reaction to this crisis is heard in their rhetoric of tradition, or as I alternately call it, their rhetoric of displacement.

Hints in what I read, especially in the trade literature, suggested that the printers' recent situation had recurrent antecedents in previous times of technological innovation, e.g., the introduction of mechanical typesetting in the late nineteenth century. Since those affected by that earlier change were not available to talk to, I felt the need to broaden my research base, reading in literary and historical sources of the period.

Economic conflicts and the printers' fight to make and maintain union work rules are carefully documented in social and labor histories. What I found in these documentary sources substantiated the things I encountered in fieldwork. In fact, things said and felt today have precedence in print more than a century earlier. The rhetoric of displacement of the late nineteenth century is remarkably similar to that of today; the printers' elitism is maintained right up to this latest and final crisis.

Ironically, the "final crisis" was resolved in what some would consider a long sought-after dream—the creation of one big union in the printing and electronics industry. President Robert S. McMichen was one of the majority of ITU affiliates who fully supported a merger in the allied printing trades. In a 1986 editorial he stressed the dramatic advance of technology, noting that "a printer of the 1950s or even 1960s would barely recognize a composing room today. As much as the technology is changing and endangering our members' jobs, so too is the increasing concentration of ownership in the communications industry. . . . Major newspaper companies have diversified into cable television and telecommunication. The result is big, powerful, sophisticated employers. The only way working people can hope to deal with them is through a big, powerful and sophisticated union."[30]

In December 1986 the International Typographical Union ceased to be. The proposed merger agreement with the Communications Workers of America was overwhelmingly approved in an ITU membership vote by over four to one. One of the costs of the merger with North America's most technologically advanced labor organization is that the ITU identity was lost. A 134-year history came to an end.

It is a history of trade identification and union strength that has naturally attracted industrial sociologists and scholars of labor relations. The best of their works bring the printers to life with a focus on the workers' experiences, implicit skills, and attitudes toward work and automation.[31] One also finds the printers' trade being compared to other craft-based industries like building,[32] and contrasted to non-craft-based industries, such as the machine-tending textile industry, the mass-production auto industry, and the continuous-process chemical industry. In his 1964 study *Alienation and Freedom,* Robert Blauner relied heavily on secondary sources, US Department of labor statistics, and the Roper survey of 1947 for his information on printers, rather than field observation of working printers.[33]

In Elizabeth Eisenstein's comprehensive study of the advent of printing, master printers are the "unsung heroes of the early-modern era," however, in her efforts to simplify cataloguing, Eisenstein chose to "refer to the tool rather than its user."[34]

Printers appear as the subjects of sociological case studies in which the specific occupation tends to be incidental to the author's stated or hidden theoretical agenda. They serve as the social scientists' vehicle for exploring the nature of collective bargaining, social stratification, and group cohesion.[35] A number of scholars find printers especially suitable for exposing the capitalist's "rationalization" of labor processes.[36] Typically, such works describe newspaper composition rooms where automation and computerization have undermined the traditional craft skills of the hand compositor and Linotype operator. Along this vein, printers have been used to argue a Marxist-feminist interpretation of a male-dominated trade.[37] In the social science researcher's attempt to define ideal types and organizational structures while preserving informants' anonymity, more often than not, the individual and the personal have been lost.

The present work attempts to add a humanistic dimension; theory is used to illuminate what makes life meaningful to the

people under study. Their material and verbal expressive forms—
those of performance and ritual as well as those extant in the little
ceremonies of everyday life—are sought out and studied for their
qualitative and quantitative significance. Texts are treated as social
fact. In contrast to the anonymous informant of sociology and an-
thropology, and the composite character of literary journalism, the
folkloristic tradition herein utilized is one of quoting people directly and at length.

You will find an abundance of texts. Practitioners of the ethnography of communication have taught us that speaking, the
nexus between language and social life, is patterned within each
society in culture-specific ways and that the patterns and functions
of speaking are discernible through ethnography.[38] In his work
with Native American texts, Dell Hymes has made a convincing
argument for the direct relationship between the form of language
use and the form of culture. He finds the patterning in narrative
texts so pervasive that it seems to embody implicit cultural schema
for the organization of experience. Patterning in oral narrative is
often marked by the recurrent use of initial grammatical particles
in sentences ("back then," "so," "now again"), the use of tense
changes, and statements of change in time or space; all have expressive as well as structural significance.[39]

Needless to say, one can only discern the patterning of discourse if texts are accurately and fully recorded. After document-
ing spoken texts in sufficient quantity, one can then place texts in
structural position to each other in order to create a meaningful
context. Retired printer Joe Malady seemed to understand. After
our chat in the lobby of the Union Printers Home in Colorado
Springs he said, "You can get the basic facts from the history
books, but the personal touch, you need to talk to people and see
what their attitudes are. . . . Eventually, when you piece these
things together, you get a picture. I'm sure that's what you're
doing."[40]

In the case of the printers, what emerges is the telling of
essentially one story in a number of permutations. I realized this
when, in the course of my quest to understand an "other's" world

of experience, their narrative accounts began to sound familiar, somewhat predictable, of a piece. One reason for this affinity, suggests Samuel Schrager, is that though uttered by individuals, "the single account belongs to an entire narrative environment. It is only by recognizing its resemblances to related accounts that we can begin to locate its traditionality."[41]

Since the narrating of experience takes shape in a social arena, the spoken memory can be heard as a verbal enactment of socially forged values and concerns. Consistency in what stories are about, congruences in the testimonies of different narrators, and significant instances of agreement in attitude and stance taken suggest that narrators are not creating their accounts for the first time simply to satisfy an ethnographic researcher. Rather, the researcher is observing and participating in a traditional and communicative process, just as she would be were she hearing fiddle tunes played or watching quilt patterns pieced.

But what to attend to? Just as not all events of the past are worth preserving in narrative form, not all testimony is worthy of study. Spend enough time with people and they will tell you what their key texts are—either directly by example or indirectly through repetition, heightened emotion, and performative speech, that is, directly quoted dialogue, the use of the present tense in referring to past events,[42] gestures, laughter, anger. To ask what the great texts are is to ask what endures, what a culture retains. Where is meaning stored, tradition reenacted, and artful work expressed? What "texts" embody the printers' pattern of thought? What key events do they chronicle, what lessons do they teach, what is most important to them? The answers to these questions lie in the culture of change; *that* is our "text"—the printer's hot-metal world, how it changed, and how this transformation has irrevocably changed the printer himself.

A Word About Transcriptions

In transcribing spoken texts from either handwritten notes or tape-recorded interviews, my primary concern has been the communication of information and affect.[43] The process of transcribing speech relies heavily on developing a good ear and a good memory. To be faithful to the tape recorder is not to create fictional dialogue, for as the writer Anthony Burgess notes, "fictional speech is more artful and economical than it appears."[44]

There are analytical and ethical considerations, as well, in any attempt to render spoken language in written form. As anyone working with oral texts knows, there exists a tension between trying to represent faithfully what was said and the temptation to edit out awkward speech, false starts, and nonsensical utterances. To complicate matters, the juxtaposition of excerpts of spoken speech with standard academic prose holds the potential danger of being read as a negative reflection on the people whose speech is being represented.[45]

When possible, I have tried to include my questions, my responses, and my ungrammatical blunders, in an effort to document the conversational context in which the interviewees' responses occurred.

In terms of typographic style I listened to Henry Glassie who stressed readability and suggested I study the novelist's handling of dialogue.[46]

Typographic symbols appearing within transcriptions are explained below:

— An em dash is used to indicate overlapping speech, e.g., a conversational juncture in which two people are talking at the same time.

. . . An ellipsis within the text indicates an omission, unless otherwise specified as a pause.

[ ] Material within square brackets has been inserted to clarify meaning.

Notes

1. Ed Jacob, former compositor at Curtis Publishing, tape-recorded interview, 30 November 1983.

2. A fermata is a musical term indicating a prolongation on a particular note or chord, beyond its given value.

3. A phrase used by Samuel Schrager in criticizing an implicit assumption of many oral historians. See "'The Early Days' Narrative and Symbolism of Logging Life in the Inland Northwest" (Ph.D. diss., University of Pennsylvania, 1983), 12.

4. The terms "cold composition," "cold type," and "cold metal" refer to any of the photocomposition or electronic typesetting processes in use today, processes that do not involve the use of molten metal.

5. Shoshana Zuboff, *The Age of the Smart Machine* (New York: Basic Books, 1988).

6. Ibid., 95.

7. A. H. Raskin, "The Negotiation: Changes in the Balance of Power," *The New Yorker*, 22 January 1979, 41.

8. As the editors of the Oxford University Press 1958 edition proclaim, Moxon's text was so useful that it was appropriated by compilers of technical encyclopedias and printers' grammars for decades to come. When subsequent advances in printing technology diminished the book's practical use, it came to be recognized as an authority for historians and hobbyists alike. Joseph Moxon, *Mechanick Exercises on the Whole Art of Printing, 1683–4,* ed. Herbert Davis and Harry Carter (Oxford: Oxford University Press, 1958).

9. Ibid., 11–12.

10. *The Compact Edition of the Oxford English Dictionary* (Oxford: Oxford University Press, 1971), 3455.

11. W. J. Rorabaugh, *The Craft Apprentice: From Franklin to the Machine Age* (New York: Oxford University Press, 1986), 78.

12. George A. Tracy, *History of the Typographical Union: Its Beginnings, Progress, and Development* (Indianapolis: International Typographical Union, 1913), 168.

13. Bertram A. Powers, president of Typographical Union No. 6, interview at No. 6 headquarters in lower Manhattan, 1 November 1985. The merger Powers refers to was finally accomplished in December 1986, but not with the printing craft unions Powers had in mind at the time (Graphic Arts International Union, which covered the pressmen). An agreement was reached between the ITU and the Communications Workers of America (CWA) which effectively ended the 134-year existence of the ITU. The ITU has become the autonomous Printing, Publishing, and Media Workers Sector of the CWA union, which, as of 1990, had 650,000 members.

14. Sandy Bevis, tape-recorded conversation in his room at the Union Printers Home in Colorado Springs, 5 February 1988. Bevis points out that though there were pressmen in the ITU they would not be residing at the

Union Printers Home as *pressmen,* per se. Bevis makes the distinction, "They weren't pressmen; they were members of the ITU . . . doing presswork. They were printers."

15. Henry Glassie, "Meaningful Things and Appropriate Myths: The Place of the Artifact in American Studies," *Prospects* (1977): 26.

16. Robert Redfield's paradigm of European folk society fails to indicate the interaction between what he calls the "great" and the "little" tradition, i.e., the civilized and literate versus the rural and unlettered. See *The Little Community* and *Peasant Society and Culture* (Chicago: University of Chicago Press, 1969).

17. Alan Dundes is generally credited with broadening the scope of folklore scholarship, to identify specifically *who* constituted the "folk" of legitimate folklore scholarship. See his introduction in *The Study of Folklore* (Englewood Cliffs, N.J.: Prentice-Hall, 1965), 2.

18. Compare oral testimony quoted throughout this work to that found in Cynthia Cockburn's study of London compositors, *Brothers: Male Dominance and Technological Change* (London: Pluto Press, 1983).

19. William McNeil, "A History of American Folklore Scholarship Before 1908" (Ph.D. diss., Indiana University, 1980).

20. Richard Handler and Jocelyn Linnekin, "Tradition: Genuine or Spurious," *Journal of American Folklore* 97 (1984): 2. Dell Hymes roots the notion not in time but in social life, using the verb "traditionalize" in place of the adjective "traditional"; see his "Folklore's Nature and the Sun's Myth," *Journal of American Folklore* 88 (1975): 353.

21. Charles L. Briggs, *Learning How to Ask: A Sociolinguistic Appraisal of the Role of the Interview in Social Science Research* (New York: Cambridge University Press, 1986), 3.

22. "Spec" type is short for specifying type elements; before manuscript copy is to be typeset, the typeface and point size must be specified, as well as whether the type will be set roman or italic, bold or light, capitalized or lower-case, etc.

23. Sigfrid H. Steinberg, *Five Hundred Years of Printing,* 3rd ed. (London: Penguin Books), 1974.

24. Tracy, *History of the Typographical Union.*

25. John W. Seybold, *World of Digital Typesetting* (Media, Pa., 1984).

26. James Moran, *Printing Presses: History and Development from the 15th Century to Modern Times* (Berkeley: University of California Press, 1978).

27. Max Kalish, *Labor Sculpture,* intro. by Emily Genauer (New York: Max Kalish, 1938), unnumbered pages.

28. Smith was fascinated with prehistoric origins of language. This totemic vertical form is an assemblage of bronze casts of found objects: the back of an

oak chair, a stool broken into parts, and a printer's type case. For more information see *David Smith,* ed. Edward F. Fry (New York: Solomon R. Guggenheim Museum, 1973), and Stanley Marcus, *David Smith: The Sculptor and His Work* (Ithaca: Cornell University Press, 1983).

29. Goudy designed classic typefaces for the American Type Foundry and the Lanston Monotype Company and authored two books: *The Alphabet* and *The Elements of Lettering.* See Warren Chappell, *A Short History of the Printed Word* (Boston: David Godine, 1980).

30. Robert S. McMichen, *Typographical Journal* (August 1986): 2. A decade of unsuccessful merger deals with the Newspaper Guild, the Graphic Communications International Union, and the Teamsters preceded the proposed merger with the Communications Workers of America. The pages of the *Typographical Journal* are full of commentary regarding the difficulties and advantages of a merger.

31. See Theresa F. Rogers and Natalie S. Friedman, *Printers Face Automation* (Lexington, Mass.: Lexington Books, 1980); Harry Kelber and Carl Schlesinger, *Union Printers and Controlled Automation* (New York: Free Press, 1967); Michael Wallace and Aarne L. Kalleberg, "Industrial Transformation and the Decline of Craft: The Decomposition of Skill in the Printing Industry," *American Sociological Review* (1982): 307–24; Cockburn, *Brothers.*

32. Mark Erlich, *With Our Own Hands: The Story of Carpenters in Massachusetts* (Philadelphia: Temple University Press, 1986). This is an excellent study of craft identity and the destruction of trade skill.

33. See Robert Blauner, *Alienation and Freedom* (Chicago: University of Chicago Press, 1964).

34. The historical implications of the shift from script to print are examined in Elizabeth Eisenstein, *The Printing Press as an Agent of Change* (Cambridge: Cambridge University Press, 1979), xv.

35. I. C. Cannon, "The Social Situation of the Skilled Worker: A Study of the Compositor in London," *Sociology* 1 (1967): 165–85.

36. See Harry Braverman, *Labor and Monopoly Capital* (New York: Monthly Review Press, 1974); Kelber and Schlesinger, *Union Printers;* Andrew Zimbalist, "Technology and the Labor Process in the Printing Industry," in *Case Studies on the Labor Process,* ed. Andrew Zimbalist (New York: Monthly Review Press, 1979); and Wallace and Kalleberg, "Industrial Transformation," 307–24.

37. Cockburn, *Brothers.*

38. Richard Bauman and Joel Sherzer, "Introduction," in *Explorations in the Ethnography of Speaking,* ed. Bauman and Sherzer (New York: Cambridge University Press, 1974).

39. See Dell Hymes, "Discovering Oral Performance and Measured Verse in American Indian Narrative," *New Literary History* 7 (1977): 431–57; and

idem, "Narrative Form as a 'Grammar' of Experience: Native Americans and a Glimpse of English," *Journal of Education* (1982): 121–42.

40. Joe Malady, retired from Atlantic City No. 337; tape-recorded interview on 2 February 1988 at the Union Printers Home in Colorado Springs.

41. Schrager, "'The Early Days.'"

42. Nessa Wolfson, "A Feature of Performed Narrative: The Conversational Historical Present," *Language and Society* 7 (1978): 215–37.

43. The majority of interviews I conducted were tape-recorded and are so indicated in the notes. In the few cases in which I used paper and pencil, the notes make no mention of a recording machine.

44. Anthony Burgess, "Modern Novels: The 99 Best, 1939–83," *New York Times Book Review,* 5 February 1984.

45. Dennis Preston, quoted by Richard Bauman, *Story, Performance, and Event: Contextual Studies of Oral Narrative,* Cambridge Studies in Oral and Literate Culture (New York: Cambridge University Press), ix.

46. See Glassie's discussion of transcription and ethnopoetics in *Passing the Time in Balleymenone* (Philadelphia: University of Pennsylvania Press, 1982), 732.

2

"It Was a World"

Old-timers

When union local president Bertram Powers reflected on the hot-metal days, he prefaced his narrative with the words, "It was a world." The conversational frame serves as a useful reminder of the importance of context; that is, meaning lies in the relation of things, not in the things themselves. This chapter will take us into the world of hot-metal printing. The man who personified this world most vividly for me is Bob Culp, a man I worked beside for eight months.[1]

The work we were hired to do had nothing to do with hot-metal composition—he proofread computer-generated copy and I pasted it up into newsletters and brochures—but our conversations had everything to do with it. They started one day in June 1985, when we experienced our second blackout of the week at work. Moments earlier Bob had stopped by my drafting table to say hello and look at my layout. We chatted about his previous work experience a bit and I asked him about the local chapter of the International Typographical Union. Jimmy O'Connor was the man to contact, a friend of Bob's, though Bob himself was no longer a dues-paying member. My supervisor came by and Bob realized that he was "keeping me from my work" and stepped back to his desk. But with the lights out, pasteup was impossible. I decided to pay him a visit.

Unlike the other employees in the university publications office, Bob Culp had hot-metal experience. His six-year apprenticeship prepared him for his work as a hand compositor, stoneman, Linotype operator, and proofreader, what is known in the trade as an all-round or practical printer. When the transition to cold composition hit the hardest, Bob was in his forties; he had made it his business to keep up with the technological changes by taking courses.

Late in the summer of 1984, Chilton Publishing had closed its West Philadelphia plant. Bob lost his mother, his son, and his job all within one month, which made being out of work all the more devastating. When months later Bob was hired as a proofreader at a university publications office, he was glad to be working again. But it was a different environment with different responsibilities and I sensed that Bob was used to higher-quality standards. We soon discovered we shared values about typographic conventions and a mutual dissatisfaction with what passed for typesetting in our midst.

At first many of our conversations were voiced in the hushed tones of mutually presumed confidentiality. But by early fall the tension lifted and he became my unofficial guide, answering queries, explaining hot-metal terminology, and telling occupational stories about practical jokes, accidents, tools, and friendships, in a relaxed manner. Curious about occupational narratives, I asked Bob, "When stories were told at work, was there a special time?" "No. This was *during* work. I was an apprentice then. This old-timer would come over and start this story. If the boss was nearby, he was only giving me instructions. As soon as the boss left, it was back to the story." Aware of the parallel to our own situation, I realized how our relationship had taken on an apprentice-master quality. I would come into work and realize he had spent time thinking up potential informants for me to talk with, "old-timers" he would call them, "people who knew the basics." Bob spoke with reverence and a warmth about those who had taught him:

"Herman Tuchinsky, a Russian Jew, he may be living in New Jersey now with his son. And Bob Campbell, he lives out in the western suburbs somewhere. I ran into him at a wedding recently. He's blind now and his wife was leading him by the arm.

"'I know that voice . . .' Campbell said.

"'It's Bob Culp, from Chilton. A stonehand that worked with you.' I turned to his wife and told her, 'He taught me a great deal of what I know about printing. He's a great teacher, so patient.'

"Tears ran down his face when he heard that."[2]

It was November when I contacted Jimmy O'Connor to ask of Herman Tuchinsky's whereabouts. "You're just a little bit too late. I got news just last week that he passed away. He was in his nineties." Two months earlier, Bob Campbell had passed away. Hot metal was a dying craft not only because it had been superseded by a new technology; its practitioners were dying.

Bob Culp took an active interest in those I did interview. I went into New York to meet with Bertram A. Powers, who, at the time, was president of the New York local of the International Typographical Union, a position he had held since 1961.[3] No. 6 is known as "Big Six" because of its reputation as the biggest and most powerful affiliate of the International Typographical Union. Powers was responsible for a series of contract ratifications in the 1960s and early 1970s which won the printers jurisdiction over manning new technology, a share in the economic benefits wrought by automation, and job security. But it was job security at a price; the bargain has been referred to as a contract of attrition, which means that the upcoming generation of printers accepts automation while the older generation accepts a retirement bonus.[4] Ironically, the issues that Powers battled in the 1980s as a union leader—manpower, controlled automation, protecting the worker—are the same issues that first captured his imagination and drew him into the printing trade.

Powers recalled: "I'll tell you what made me go into it. I was about twelve at the time. I overheard my two uncles talking. They were pressmen. One said to the other, 'You know, they've got a machine now that can set type *without* the printer, and they've put the patent in the safe! Now *that's* a union.'

"That sounded pretty good to me. The trouble was, there was no patent in the safe."[5]

Powers's ability to negotiate union contracts is admired by

Fig. 4. Bob Culp at his desk, December 1985. Photo by the author.

many. A printer in Rogers and Friedman's study, *Printers Face Automation,* is quoted as saying, "The new contract [1974] is a beauty. The question is: How did he do it without a gun?"[6] Junius Scales, standing member of the ITU, spoke highly of Powers and the union:

"That's *my* union, ITU. I was in the clean part of the business. I was a proofreader—worked at jobshops, and at the *Times* in New York. We had a great union leader at our Local, No. 6. Bert Powers: a great trade unionist. He's the best trade unionist

Fig. 5. Cover of *Time*, 1 March 1963. Copyright 1963 Time Inc. Reprinted by permission.

since Harry Bridges of the Longshoremen's Union [ILWU]. Oh, it was a beautiful contract."[7]

When I mentioned this powerful man to Bob Culp, he knew of him. "Oh, Bertram Powers, that's a big name in union politics. How'd your interview go?" I told him about it, how after Powers had finished talking about his professional concerns of union organization, wages, security, and technology, he leaned back in his chair and reminisced.

"It was a world . . .

"It smelled of oil, the lead—always a slight burning smell . . ." Powers raised both hands and fingered the air.

". . . and you'd burn your fingers on the hot metal.

"But we liked it. You were working with your hands. And you worked with each other. Brothers—you had to work together. You had something to do with the entire project. Not so now.

"We were printers. Printers hung around with printers."

He paused there, as if for emphasis in juxtaposing two worlds: then and now. After a moment, he continued.

"We have more women working today. And people don't stay on. In ad [advertising] houses, they come and go.

"It's a new breed of cat. They don't raise families. They smoke pot."

He smiled.

"Our guys drank booze, of course. They were different. Not better, mind you, just different. The pride's gone."

As I relayed to Bob Culp what I had learned from Bertram Powers about the conditions under which printers worked, the smell of the ink, the heat, how they would burn their fingers on the hot slugs, Bob was stirred to interrupt me.

"You don't know what this means to me. You're not even aware of it."

He gestured with his hands, mimicking my own, which had just fingered imaginary slugs from the Linotype machine.

"We could take those slugs, fresh out of the Linotype, and not burn ourselves, balancing them just right."

Through the reporting of occupational narrative, one printer had been emotionally connected to another in the brotherhood of their trade.

The printer's nostalgia narrative evokes occupation-specific elements of an era gone by: the sensuality and risk involved in working with raw materials, the loyalty and pleasures that sustain fellowship, the tough times tempered by pride and satisfaction in a job well done.

Powers's contrast of the "then" of hot metal with the "now" of the present follows the pattern of other golden age narratives, a genre common within occupational folklore.[8] Retired steelworkers idealize the pre-automation, pre-union era as a time when workers felt greater pride in their jobs and a sense of loyalty to the company. They boast of a willingness and capacity to work double shifts at the coke plant.[9] Retired black railroad laborers talk with pride of the care taken in maintaining track beds with blood, sweat, and tears, before mechanization depleted their ranks.[10] Commercial fishermen glorify the "old days" as a time of wooden ships and iron men. "Today, the ships are built of steel and the men of lesser stuff."[11] Policemen have a similar saying, "Iron men with wooden sticks have become wooden men with iron sticks."

Folklorists Timothy Lloyd and Pat Mullen characterize the telling of then and now narratives as a nostalgia for the "good old bad old days." Country singer Dolly Parton put the notion to music back in 1969 with her song "The Good Old Days (When Times Were Bad)."

How bad times become good times for those remembering them is, in large part, what this book is about.

Dirt and Squirts: Working Conditions

It was not a neat or clean world. The working conditions of the printers' craft are documented in labor statistics, described in trade journals, depicted in literary passages, and lampooned in cartoons. More than one informant has spoken to me of the harsh working conditions, the heat, the noise, the smell and feel of burning lead.

A thirty-four-year veteran of the Government Printing Office writes of the Linotype section at the GPO, during the 1930s. At age eighty, he titles his column "Deserving Pensioners."

> There were 96 Linotype machines, each holding a pot of 600-degree molten metal, giving forth lead fumes into the air we were breathing. . . . Over each make-up bank there were six 100-watt electric light bulbs under brass reflectors and they were so hot that a type slug, if laid on any one of them, would melt and drip onto the bank. There was no air conditioning and the only electric fan in the section sat on the floor by the foreman's desk.
>
> There were a number of open hand-type racks in the room and their cases were contaminated with cockroach and mouse excreta and lead dust. .
>
> On each of the four proof presses in the section there was a dispenser containing benzine, a toxic solvent, used in cleaning printer's ink from type, and it not only was poisonous to the handler, but also contributed to the contamination of the atmosphere.[12]

This man's remembrances of fifty years ago are reiterated in fictional accounts of the time. Albert Halper's 1934 novel *The Foundry* captures the atmosphere of a 1928 Chicago electrotype foundry where printing plates were made.

> The hot fierce sun beat down upon the skylights and soaked the men in perspiration. . . .
>
> But at last the working day was over, and the five o'clock bell rang out. The men sat tired on their stools, waiting for the ache to leave their backs, then made their way to the long wash-up trough, shouldering each other in silence. Their hands, coarsened and calloused by years of contact with the plates, were yellow and horny inside the palms but sensitive and soft at the fingertips. They washed up like beasts, sloshing themselves. The molders, black from the graphite lead, stripped to the waist and splashed themselves, and their navels, their ears, and the insides of their nostrils were as black as bullet holes, even after washing.

Fig. 6. Union Printers Home, circa 1912. Photo by A. James Harlan.

They rubbed their bodies with dirty towels and what bodies they had![13]

Conditions in the composing room—kerosene lamps, fumes from melting lead and decomposing ink, poor ventilation, dust arising from cuttings of type metal, and the ubiquity of a common towel and drinking cup—exacerbated health problems.[14] Life expectancy for ITU members at the turn of the century was forty-one years. Pulmonary tuberculosis was rampant in the printing trades.[15]

The need for a union home to house infirm and aged printers was first discussed by union delegates at an 1857 national convention. It took decades of discussion, planning, and a generous gift of $10,000 from two Philadelphia publishers, Anthony Drexel and George Childs, to make the idea of a home a reality. A donation of prairie land from the Colorado Springs Board of Trade helped get the project off the ground. The balance of the construction costs were met with union-member contributions.[16]

Fig. 7. Model of oxygen tent. Photo by A. James Harlan.

Initially the Printers Home was established as a place to care for those suffering from occupational disease.[17] Colorado's Rocky Mountains were the nineteenth-century American mecca for those seeking a cure from tuberculosis. Oxygen tents were set up on the grounds behind the main building of the home. In 1939, a sanitorium was built for the sole purpose of treating pulmonary disease.

When the home was first constructed in 1891, it cost $70,000. Today, a century later, the building's roughcut buff and red sandstone, its symmetrical weathervaned turrets, and its neo-Gothic ornamental motifs carved in stone stand as emblems of architectural grandeur of an era gone by. Like the craft of printing itself, the home's heyday flourished in an earlier age.

An arched gateway frames the entrance to the home—a monument unto itself. Bronze letters splayed across the sandstone arch read, "Union Printers Home: Its Bounty Unpurchasable, Its Charity without Price."

Agricultural and horticultural activity once produced enough sustenance for residents and staff. A 1938 inventory lists farm and stock equipment; livestock including mulch cows, heifers, Holsteins, horses, goats, bulls, boars, and sows; a poultry department; a dairy barn complete with milking machinery, churn, and cream separator; a carpentry shop; laundry; butcher shop; and paint shop. In addition to a working farm, the grounds included areas that were manicured in style. A guest dining room was equipped with lace runners, pink cocktail glasses, and oyster forks—most likely reserved for visiting union officials.

Though the home's formal gardens, greenhouses, bakery, and dairy barn with its prizewinning herds no longer exist, the grandiose main building does. A museum, picture albums, and endless halls hung with panoramic photographs of successive national conventions put residents and visitors in mind of the past, when printers wore high hats and considered themselves aristocracy among labor craftspeople.

The best reminder of this esteemed past is the oral testimony of the home's current residents, printers from across the United States and Canada who are eager to share their collective experi-

Fig. 8. Arched entrance to the Union Printers Home, 1988. Photo by the author.

Fig. 9. Bakery. Photo by A. James Harlan.

Fig. 10. Formal gardens. Photo by A. James Harlan.

ences of the craft and the union that sustain them. It was an ITU member who first suggested the value of a visit to the Union Printers Home in Colorado Springs. "Go out there, they'll talk your ears off," Ed Jacobs had said. And talk they did.

I spent a week in the company of men and women, many of whom got their start in the trade by handsetting copy in small country print shops. A few told personal narratives of being tramp printers, traveling the country on rails. Most spent the majority of their working days tapping out copy on Linotype machines. The average age of residents is seventy-seven, indicating that many got out of the trade before the revolution of computer-aided typesetting.

At one time a horse-drawn wagon was the only transportation down the hill to town. In the 1920s a trolley line replaced the horsepower. Today there are buses and vans that take the residents on shopping and sightseeing excursions.

Fig. 11. Residents enjoying a poker game, 1988. Photo by the author.

Looking out from the home's expansive front lawn, one can see Pike's Peak, rising some fourteen thousand feet to the northeast, framed by the monumental arched gateway. The view beyond the gateway is a joy to most residents. Back east, however, the view is infamous. When I mention the mountain's beauty to Bertram Powers, president of New York's Big Six, the diehard New Yorker answers, "Yeah, if you like that sort of thing. We have a joke about it. This old guy from Brooklyn was living out there with Pike's Peak right out his window. Somebody asked him, 'How do you like your room?' He responded, 'It's fine. If only they'd remove that mountain, you might have a view.'"

The joke hints at what may have been big-city printers' reservations about residing at a rest home situated in such an unfamiliar landscape. Though all union members knew they were entitled to the benefits of the home, did any of them actually expect to end up there?

A resident of the home shows me a photograph taken nineteen years earlier, when he was elected an organizational representative. "That's when I used to come visit the Printers Home. I

Fig. 12. Horse-drawn transportation to town. Photo by A. James Harlan.

thought, 'Hell, that's a nice place to be.' But I never thought *I'd* be here." I ask another resident, Clifford Gallant, if, as a younger man, he had ever thought he might come out to the home.

He shakes his head. "No one does."

"What was the feeling about this place, when you were younger and you were working? You knew it existed, right?"

"I'm never going to be old," Clifford says. The answer seems so obvious, once it is enunciated. He continues. "That's the attitude of the average person. Yeah, you're never going to be old. Same way as 'I'm never going to retire either.' When you're sixty-five, you do.

"No, the average printer never gave it a thought that he would be coming here. I *knew* fellows that came, but there was no reason in my being here. My other brother was a printer. And he said, 'When I used to pay my dues, I never thought that someone in our family would be here.'" [18]

Once printers found themselves living at the home, attitudes were likely to change. One very appreciative resident, sent to the home due to illness, corresponds with her local in Tampa, Florida.

Colorado Springs, Colorado
Union Printers Home
July 12, 1947

My dear Mr. Zeigler -

I was very tired when I got here, but with nothing to do but rest, I am normal again.

The project here is a continual wonder to me. The immensity of the thing and the smoothness with which it operates.

I have seen several doctors but have not asked for a verdict yet. The neurologist is the only one who has prescribed for me.

Please thank No. 299 for me in making it possible for me to be here.

My best wishes go to everyone.

Sincerely and Fraternally,
Emma Langdale

Colorado Springs, Colo
Aug. 15, 1947

Mr. J. A. Zeigler, Sec'y
Tampa T.U. No. 299,
Tampa, Fla-

Dear Mr. Zeigler,

Thanks many times for the check, but my needs are well taken care of by the home and being a simple person, I desire few luxuries. The ones I do indulge myself are amply covered by the check I receive from the Tribune. I hope to see you sometime in September. I am feeling much better and really the care given here is very good. I have nothing but praise for the consideration given me.

Thanks again -[19]

It is over forty years since these letters were written, and the printers' home continues to provide care for union members. The Home Endowment Fund is proof of the pride and deep affection felt by working printers toward the home. A number of printers left their entire estates of tens of thousands of dollars to the home. Until fairly recently, the home annually received hundreds of unsolicited contributions from printers or their families.[20]

The home operates as a licensed general hospital and long-term care facility. Inside the main building are administrative offices, a pharmacy, a barber shop, a library, and recreation and dining rooms. The four floors for residents are designated "skilled," "intermediate," and "independent"—hospital lingo which specifies the degree of nursing care required on each floor. Residents on the ground floor have the most mobility, their afflictions allowing. Broken hips are as common as bingo games.

A long hallway is flanked by residents' rooms on each side. Walking down the corridor of mostly open doors, one notices hospital beds and minimal furniture, radios and televisions playing, personalized touches: a crucifix on the wall, a crocheted afghan, color snapshots tacked to cork bulletin boards, not unlike some college dormitories. At the same time, it is like walking down a hospital corridor where one is tempted to avert one's eyes, not wanting to invade privacy or see tubes and medical equipment and suffering.

An open door reveals three elderly men congregated in one man's room, sitting around, one in a chair, one on the bed, and one in a wheelchair, shooting the breeze, telling stories, laughing. I realize that these are not just old men in a nursing home, but that they are old *printers* in their own union home.

One of the first residents I am introduced to is Neil "Angelface" Fuller, age ninety-eight, and the unofficial oral historian of the home. A few years older than the home itself, Neil Fuller spent many of his working years laboring under kerosene lamps. He is never at a loss for conversation, only words—somebody's name, a town, a year—but his talk flows easily.

Neil is proud of the home in a proprietary way. A leather recliner in the lobby is his perch. He misses nothing, including the backdoor entrance of the undertaker come to carry away the deceased. This nonagenarian is trusted with the keys to the home's museum and is a keeper of tradition.

Fig. 13. Neil "Angelface" Fuller, 1988. Photo by the author.

Printers are well aware of their own history. As an occupational group, they are committed to extolling the union's historic role in securing better working conditions, fair wages, job security, and a final resting place for ITU members. Amelia Story, an eighty-one-year-old resident, discusses the commonly held belief behind the home's existence: "People used to put printers in basements with no ventilation. In those days, why they were just treated like animals. They developed TB. That's why this place was built. Because so many of our people developed TB. . . . To this day, I still think that union was the best thing that ever happened to the working man."[21]

And the working woman. It appears to me, not yet an historian of American unionism, that the ITU led the way in establishing women's rights in the workplace. In 1869 women were granted the right to join existing unions and to form unions of their own. It was resolved, four years later, that all subordinate unions were recommended to admit female printers to membership upon the same footing, in all respects, as males.[22] This meant that women were to earn the same scale and work under the same conditions as men. Though they number one-quarter of the male population in the home, the women residents are here as living proof of their right to work.

"I've always been proud to be a printer," Amelia Story tells me. "And I've even had people turn up their nose, 'Oh, printer.' I said, 'You bet a printer. And a good one too.'"[23]

Union pride is evident in material culture as well. On the top of a museum case sits a paper replica of the Union Printers Home, painstakingly pieced together by a resident. A drawer in a nearby case holds a two-dimensional representation, made entirely from canceled postage stamps.

Such gestures of iconography are treasured as museum objects, but are not limited to museum interiors. The clock on the central tower of the home is permanently set at eight o'clock to commemorate the union's struggle in securing the eight-hour workday—a triumph won in 1907.[24] The hands of the tower clock have remained at eight o'clock ever since.

Fig. 14. Amelia Story and Hazel Orth, 1988. Photo by the author.

This ritual stopping of time and the building of commemorative models are living tributes to earlier generations' ideals and accomplishments. For the retired and the infirm printer who spent a lifetime associating with an honorable craft, the home is a supportive environment, both physically and emotionally.

Dying, however, is a daily fact of life at the home. As a resident, Fil Valdez, wrote to me in 1988, "Things are rolling along as usual. Some die and others are admitted, so from time to time we've got a whole new group of people." [25]

To live and die among kindred spirits is a form of "social security" that breathes new life into an American birthright since 1935. Unfortunately, the security of a rest home is now threatened by the very same forces that displaced printers from their Linotypes and eliminated the need for their specialized skills. Technology has brought the computer and telecommunications to the world of printing in a big way. The 1986 merger with the Communications Workers of America has ended the ITU's existence. On the eve of its centenary, the future of the Union Printers Home is uncertain.

Fig. 15. Home exterior, 1988. Photo by the author.

Fig. 16. Model of the home exterior. Photo by the author.

Fig. 17. Clock tower, 1988. Photo by the author.

In a letter dated 16 December 1988, Fil Valdez wrote, ". . . I vacated the home on Oct. 15 but all my mail was forwarded to my home. . . .

"Joe Malady passed away the last week of Sept. and 'Angel Fuller' and Lloyd Hovde passed away on the same day in November. I vacated and Cliff Gallant vacated so there is a complete new bunch of residents on the first floor.

"I've had a difficult time adjusting to family living, but I'm sure things will straighten up.

"Things are not looking too good for the home. Not many

Fig. 18. Union Printers Home cemetery. Photo by Jim Bates.

people are coming in and the enrollment is way down. When I went there 22 months ago, there were 147 and last week it was down to 115.

"On Nov. 1st they raised the assessment (rent) to $500, an increase of $250 which I could not handle so I vacated. I have not heard of how it's affecting some of those people. I know some of them *cannot* pay that much.

"All we can do is wait and watch for whatever plans they can come up with.

"I sure miss that place. Those peaceful surroundings are priceless. When I go for walks here, all I breathe are exhaust fumes. . . ."

The poor working conditions that first inspired the building of the Union Printers Home persisted well into the twentieth century. Up until the 1930s, many printing plants lacked adequate washing facilities. Cold water, if there was water at all, could not wash the accumulation of lead, ink, and grease from workers' hands, the same hands that handled sandwiches at lunchtime, brought from home. To make matters worse, it was customary for workers to share a common towel. The existence of this communal towel has inspired creative expression through the years, examples of which appeared in the pages of the popular trade journal, the *Inland Printer.*

The Printer's Towel

When I think of the towel,
The old-fashioned towel,
That used to hang up by the printing-house door.
I think that nobody,
In these days of shoddy,
Can hammer out iron to wear as it wore.

The tramp who abused it,
The devil who used it,
The comp. who got at it when these two were gone.
The makeup and foreman
The editor, poor man,
Each rubbed some grime off for the heap they put on.

In, over, and under,
'Twas harder than poverty, rougher than sin.
From the roller suspended,
It never was bended,
And flapped on the wall like a banner of tin.

It grew thicker and rougher,
And harder and tougher,
And daily put on a more inkier hue;
Until, one windy morning,
Without any warning,
It fell on the floor and was broken in two.

—Burnette[26]

In the foreword to a book entitled *The Tramp Printer,* the communal towel is further immortalized: "The ancient and disreputable office towel . . . stood its position more sturdily almost than some of the improvised tables that supported imposing stones. Running water was unknown, and the water which was provided was used over and over again for ablutionary purposes

"In the Days That Wuz"—The Old-Fashioned Towel
Cartoon by John T. Nolf, Printer-Artist

Fig. 19. The old-fashioned towel. Drawn by John T. Nolf for the *Inland Printer*, January 1926. Reprinted from the *Inland Printer* with permission of *American Printer*/Maclean Hunter Publishing Co. All rights reserved.

until it acquired a soupy consistency."[27] Later on in the text of this small book we are informed that "the towel would stand without assistance in a corner of the room, such was its incrustation of antique grime and neolithic ink."[28]

The infamous towel is illustrated in John T. Nolf's cartoon (fig. 19) which appeared in the January 1927 issue of the *Inland Printer.*

Poor working conditions recorded in documentary sources are corroborated in oral testimony. Stories circulate of grisly accidents, hot-lead burns, and hazardous chemicals:

"Every department, from composing to bindery, had its dangers. I saw a guy lose three fingers from here forward." Bob Culp points to the first joint of his left hand, where the index finger meets the palm.

"It was in the pressroom. He was working on a 6–o flatbed. It was in the middle of the night and they took him to Misericordia Hospital. A surgeon, who was also a nun, met us there. 'Where are his fingers? He's a young man. Go find them.'

"They rushed back from the hospital, which was on Fifty-sixth and Chestnut, and looked all over. They found them. They were in the *ink!* They fished them out—they were all black, blue, whatever color they were running that night.

"She spent hours on him. This was before micro surgery was even heard of. It took a long time but he got some mobility back." [29]

Even if a printer managed to keep all his fingers, there were other occupational health hazards. Jim Spurlock, a Kentucky-born, Chicago printer in his late fifties, recalls the comp room at the *Chicago Times:* "You're sitting there at a Linotype with a gas pot under it, the metal melting and the fumes coming off of it. You can't help but breathe some of it in." Jim's pal, Frank Koncel, a fellow member of No. 16 in Chicago, also worked at the *Chicago Tribune.* He adds, "See, when you were working with the Ludlow [a linecasting machine used primarily for setting headlines], the pot in front of you was 550 degrees. To keep the metal molten."

Jim's Kentucky drawl overpowers Frank's gravelly voice. "The Linotype was 535. And if some of that splashed on you, boy, you could just peel the meat off. It didn't burn you, it cooked you. That's what they called a squirt."

"Squirts, yeah," Frank adds. "Sometimes you were setting a loose line . . ." But Jim interrupts and finishes Frank's sentence.

"Setting a loose line, when your mats turned sideways and

the plunger went down, that left a hole, oh, about a half an inch by an inch. Boom! That metal'll just come right through there." Jim points to his left eye. "I know that's the reason I got half of my eye gone. I got some hit me right there."[30]

Two women residents of the Printers Home have their own share of squirt stories. The scars from burns that Amelia Story has are mostly healed over. Nothing as serious as her next-door neighbor, Hazel Orth, who tells us of an accident she experienced.

"I was in the hospital with my arms submerged in water solution." Though she is somewhat frail in frame, Hazel has a lifetime smoker's deep voice that gives her a commanding presence. She speaks slowly.

"I was working at a small place. Only one machine. And it had snowed. And evidently, someone came in walking around there and snow spilled off in one of those pigs. Those long pigs you had to hang up," she explains, "that went down into the metal pot."

"And I went to put one of those on and the thing just exploded. And I had a wool dress on and a smock on over that. And once it hit the wool, why, I'd had it."[31]

Less dramatic yet equally nocuous substances, like the toxic solvent used to clean type, are remembered by printers, but are often belittled as in Bob Culp's talk. "Benzine. Nasty stuff. We'd use that to clean off the ink." I tell Bob about the time I telephoned the Union Rubber Company, manufacturers of the solvent, and asked them for the chemical contents. A woman at work had been developing a rash and I was concerned about the product's toxicity.

Bob reassures me, "I handled so much at one time and I seem to be okay. The amount I handled you could *swim* in."

"You didn't wear gloves?"

"Gloves?! That would be like making cookies with boxing gloves on."[32]

On noise: "If you got a couple of dozen Linotypes running it was real noisy," says Jim Spurlock. "Well, if you had ten cars sitting here and all of them had a little motor trouble, you're going to have a lot of noise. We had one gal come to work and sit down. She'd put a pair of ear muffs on. That'd tell you how noisy it was."

Jim sighs and Frank complements the sigh with a "Yap."[33]

Talk of noxious fumes, enervating noise, and occupational accidents is nearly always accompanied and balanced by conciliatory statements that make it all seem worth it—times-were-tough-but-we-enjoyed-it kind of talk.

If some took the printing world to the grave with them, most took it home. Bob Culp recalls his work at Chilton: "In the heat of the summer, we'd be covered with sweat from head to foot. At the end of the day you'd go over to the fountain, you'd strip down to your waist and just let the water run over you. I'd come home and my wife would say, 'I smell Chilton, Hon. I smell Chilton.' We worked so hard trying to make a work of art out of it. It wasn't peaches and cream. We were exhausted at the end of our shifts, but satisfied. In a way that's gone today. The pride."[34]

How did such a dirty, hot, and noisy world—a world where printers could lose fingers and hands—come to be such a source of fond reminiscence and pride? There is no simple answer. It might be better to ask what this former world of work has come to symbolize. To do that, we must first recreate that world, which is what happens during most conversations with those who lived in it.

Notes

1. As a graduate student I had a part-time position in the production department of the university publications office. At the time, Culp was employed there as a proofreader.

2. Bob Culp, former stoneman and Linotype operator at Chilton Publishing, personal communication, 21 June 1985.

3. Bertram Powers retired from his No. 6 presidency in June 1990.

4. For information on Bertram Powers's role in union politics see Kelber and Schlesinger, *Union Printers and Controlled Automation;* A. H. Raskin, "The Negotiation," 22 and 29 January 1979; and Rogers and Friedman, *Printers Face Automation.*

5. Bertram A. Powers, president, International Typographical Union No.

6, interview, 1 November 1985. Historically, the ITU has resisted technological innovations that might displace printers from their jobs.

6. Rogers and Friedman, *Printers Face Automation,* 107.

7. Junius Scales, former Communist, convicted under the membership clause of the Smith Act. Mr. Scales mentioned that while he was working at the *Times* the FBI had tried repeatedly to take away his union card. Bert Powers stood by him; Scales said, "He'd have nothing of it." Personal communication at the Southern Historical Association annual meeting, 14 November 1986.

8. Jack Santino has found the following to be pervasive in the storytelling of workers: hostility toward authority, first-day-on-the-job stories, golden age narratives, cautionary tales, pranks and trickster tales, and legends of heroic feats. See his "Characteristics of Occupational Narrative," in *Working Americans: Contemporary Approaches to Occupational Folklife,* ed. Robert Byington, Smithsonian Folklife Studies No. 3 (Los Angeles: California Folklore Society, 1978), 57–70.

9. See Richard M. Dorson, *Land of the Millrats* (Cambridge, Mass.: Harvard University Press, 1981), 47–50.

10. Field research with retired black railroad workers in Alabama and Mississippi during 1988.

11. Commercial fisherman quoted by Timothy Lloyd and Patrick Mullen, "Occupational Identity: Commercial Fishermen on Lake Erie;" paper delivered at the Southern Anthropological Society annual meeting, Wrightsville Beach, North Carolina, 26 April 1986. See their book, *Lake Erie Fishermen: Work, Identity, and Tradition* (Urbana: University of Illinois Press, 1990), especially 79–92. Recurring themes in the stories of these midwestern retired fishermen include starting-out experiences, family tradition, and a contrast between the past and the present.

The style of occupational nostalgia will be taken up in more detail in chapter 7.

12. Clifford L. Schneider, "Deserving Pensioners," *Typographical Journal* 75 (May 1985): 74.

13. Albert Halper, *The Foundry* (New York: Viking, 1934), 28 and 292.

14. See Jacob Loft, *The Printing Trades* (New York: Farrar and Rinehart, 1944), for a depiction of the hazards a printer encountered in his daily work.

15. Lydia Avery, *Saga ITU Oldtimers + Printers Home,* undated, unpaged. Avery was a member of the ITU for seventy years.

16. Tracy, *History of the Typographical Union.*

17. Tuberculosis took its toll among pressroom workers as well. The International Printing Pressmen and Assistants' Union followed the plan adopted by the ITU. In 1910, a home was constructed in the mountains of eastern Tennessee as a refuge for the pressmen's union's ill and aged members. Like the Union Printers Home in Colorado, the Pressmen's Home included ample acreage for

cultivation and livestock. See Elizabeth F. Baker, *Printers and Technology* (New York: Columbia University Press, 1957), 316–19.

18. Clifford Gallant, Bay Area No. 21, tape-recorded interview in his room at the Union Printers Home, 5 February 1988.

19. Correspondence of Emma Langdale to the secretary of her local, No. 299 of Tampa, Florida. Used courtesy of The Southern Labor Archives (Box 634, No. 7), Georgia State University.

20. Carl Schlesinger, personal communication, February 1990.

21. Amelia Story, Cleveland No. 53, tape-recorded interview in her room at the Union Printers Home, 3 February 1988.

22. Tracy, *History of the Typographical Union.*

23. Amelia Story, interview, 3 February 1988.

24. The eight-hour day was established in the book and job branches of the printing industry in 1901. Efforts began in 1903 to establish these hours for all branches of the industry. See Tracy, *History of the Typographical Union.*

25. Fil Valdez, letter dated 22 August 1988.

26. *Inland Printer* 76, no. 4 (January 1926): 572. Note that in stanza 2, "tramp" refers to a tramp printer, an itinerant journeyman who traveled from job to job, on the strength of his union card, and stayed as long as the work lasted. "Devil" is another word for the printer's apprentice.

27. Ben Hur Lampman, *The Tramp Printer, Sometime Journeyman of the Little Home-Town Papers in Days that Come No More,* foreword by Elbert Bede (Portland, Ore.: Metropolitan Press, 1934), 6.

28. Ibid., 33.

29. Bob Culp, personal communication, 13 December 1985.

30. Tape-recorded conversation with Jim Spurlock and Frank Koncel, two residents of the Union Printers Home in Colorado Springs, 2 February 1988.

31. Tape-recorded conversation with Amelia Story and Hazel Orth, two residents of the Union Printers Home in Colorado Springs, 3 February 1988.

32. Bob Culp, personal communication, 4 November 1985.

33. Spurlock and Koncel, tape-recorded conversation, 2 February 1988.

34. Culp, personal communication, 4 November 1985.

3

Terms, Tools, Techniques, and Tales

The majority of early conversations and interviews I had with printers tended to focus on occupational jargon. In doing so they served as extended explications of outmoded trade terms and processes. I was learning, and the printers took the responsibility very seriously. Misuse of terminology was and is not tolerated. It is as if hot-metal terminology is sacred, an occupational argot with a diminishing speech population. Those remaining speakers are compelled toward conservative usage. Despite their efforts, technological change has brought on a metaphorization of shoptalk.

As printing technology has moved further and further away from the hands-on craft of carpentry and lead, a comparable shift in language has occurred. The transition from hot type to cold type is paralleled by a move from literal to metaphoric language. Terms that once referred to tangible items now refer to processes. "Leading" no longer means the actual strips of lead alloy spacing material placed between lines of cast type, it means the process of optically creating "white space" by keyboarding at a video display terminal, with no lead in sight.

Pursuing the archaeology of the printer's occupational jargon leads to history, aesthetics, and a way of remembering process. Trade jargon is like an oral form of shorthand; it is only meaningful to those trained to use it. Trade-specific terminology is therefore a useful entry point of investigation—terms so practical everyone working in the field knows what they mean, yet so ephemeral, so tied to the times and the technology at hand, that their meanings and derivations run the risk of getting lost in time or being appropriated for new techniques.

Early Customs

As a trade with a long history, printing is alive with occupation-specific folklore—technical language, legendary heroes, initiation rites, gestures, and foodways customs—many of which can be traced back over three centuries. For example, the customs of the chapel. It might seem odd that the composition room of a big-city newspaper circa 1980 would have a chapel, unless one knows that "chapel" designates not a place of worship but the union shop to which the printers belong.

The "father" or chairman of the chapel is responsible for ensuring equitable distribution of work, the scheduling of shifts to guarantee compliance with the contract, and the settling of disputes. Retired printer Joe Malady describes the chapel as a branch of the local union:

"They had meetings and the chapel chairman usually set the criterion on what was the invasion of the union rights. He was the judge on whether you were keeping up the standard that the union set for that place. So actually, he was the boss of the printers. Aside from the foreman and the manager, he settled disputes like differences of scale and the case of overlapping work on nightshift or dayshift." [1]

Retired stonehand Tony Donaghy was elected chairman of the composing room at Chilton Publishing in Philadelphia for twelve consecutive years. He recalls: "It doesn't mean you're holding office. You are the boss of the printers in the place." Fellow workers Bob Culp and Dan Burns told me of Donaghy's perseverance in insisting the union provide better health care for one of its members. [2]

The meaning of "chapel" as a democratic organization of printers dates back well before the seventeenth century. "Every *Printing-house*," Moxon informs us, "is by the Custom of Time out of mind called a *Chappel:* and all the Workmen that belong to it are *Members of the Chappel:* and the Oldest Freeman is *Father of the Chappel.*"[3]

Some pose an ecclesiastical origin for the designation of "chapel,"[4] but by the mid-twentieth century, any clerical connection was remote, and in the following case, a source of humorous verse.

The Printer's Chapel

The printer's chapel is a nebulous thing:
The printer does not pray, nor does he sing.
No psalm is told, no devotion read,
Nor within its close is any soul led.

Lady printers, here excluded, eagerly suspect
That what transpires within is not circumspect.[5]

The chapel originally functioned both as an association of self-government and as a subscription fund for treats. The workmen (master printers and apprentices excluded) agreed to abide by certain rules and customs for the good of the chapel, i.e., the workmen of the printing office. Swearing, fighting, singing, drunkenness, and the use of abusive language were offenses, for which penalties were imposed. Judgment was rendered by a plurality of chapel-member votes.

The penalty for the breach of any of these laws or customs was called "solace." According to the *Oxford English Dictionary* the usage of "solace" as a noun meaning "penalty" and a verb meaning "to punish" is confined to the printing trade. The *OED* finds only two citations besides Moxon for this usage, one in an 1888 printer's vocabulary and the other in a letter written by Benjamin Franklin. It is curious that a word, which in general usage meant "to console" or "to alleviate discomfort," would take on the opposite meaning within the printing trade and nowhere else. If the purpose of solacing was an attempt to maintain orderly conduct among the workmen, then it was the others, not the offender, who would have been consoled by the solacing.

Attentiveness on the job was encouraged by chapel law. It

was a punishable offense for a compositor to drop his composing stick and let another pick it up, for three letters and a space to be found under a compositor's case, for a pressman to leave his blankets in the tympan[6] at noon or night, and for any workman to leave a candle burning at night. The latter rule undoubtedly decreased the risk of fire in the printing house.

Goofing around had its price. Men were fined for throwing things and for splashing water at each other in the pressroom, for the sensible reason that the paper would be dirtied and ruined.[7]

Solaces had to be bought off, the amount of which varied according to the nature of the offense. In days past, if the delinquent refused to pay his fine, he was corporally punished, and rather brutally so. Moxon recorded one such event: "The Workmen take him by force, and lay him on his Belly athwart the *Correcting-stone,* and held him there while another of the Workmen, with a Paper-board, gave him . . . Eleven blows on his Buttocks; which he laid on according to his own mercy. For Tradition tells us, that about 50 years ago one was *Solaced* with so much violence, that he presently Pissed Blood, and shortly after dyed of it."[8]

There were less direct ways of persuading a man to conform to chapel customs. Those who violated chapel rules were socially ostracized, often through the playing of practical jokes. Any mischief done to the resistant party was done secretly and attributed to "Ralph" or "The Spirit." William Savage, author of a nineteenth-century printing dictionary, explains: "Every chapel is haunted by an imaginary spirit, named Ralph; and when any person refuses to obey its mandates, this spirit begins to *walk,* as it is termed. The first act is, in general, to hide the offender's composing stick; if this does not answer, his galleys are secreted; then the page cords, which secure his work, are cut, and his labour rendered more than useless, because he has to distribute his pie [a jumbled mess of type] as well as recompose his matter. . . ."[9] The charade escalated until the offender was prevented from continuing his work.

A stranger venturing into the printers' domain was considered fair game for solacing. According to Moxon, if anyone entered the king's printing house asking for a ballad, or came into any printing office enquiring whether a compositor had news of a galley at sea, he or she was charged with a fine.[10] We can be sure that women entered seventeenth-century printing houses because a solace was due a workman who saluted a woman in the chapel.

It was a punishable offense for workmen to talk of spending chapel money until Saturday night, or even to mention pooling their money to send out for drink. A solace was in order if one excited any of the chapel to play at quadrats for either money or drink. The latter diversion was a form of gambling, or typographic crap shooting, only instead of dice the journeymen tossed quadrats (pieces of type metal lower in height than types, so as to leave a blank space when printed). Moxon describes how "they take five or seven m *Quadrats* holding their Hand below the Surface of the *Correcting Stone,* shake them in their Hand, and toss them upon the *Stone,* and then count how many *Nicks*[11] upwards each man throws in three times, or any other number of times agreed on: And he that throws most Wins the Bett of all the rest and stands out free. . . ."[12]

Jeffing, as this form of gambling came to be known, survived in some printing houses until relatively recently. At the *Evening Recorder* office in Amsterdam, New York, during the 1940s, compositors were known to gather around the imposing stone at the end of the working day to "jeff for a scuttle of suds."[13] Journeymen not only jeffed for beer, but to settle practical matters. An 1871 dictionary of typography states that journeymen jeffed to decide who would get the good or "fat" jobs to set.[14] This form of jeffing was not the practice in New York City, at least not in recent times. Journeyman printer Carl Schlesinger recalls that sheets of copy to be set were placed one on top of another. A union printer was supposed to take a job off the top of the pile and complete it, regardless of whether it was difficult or easy. Doing otherwise was frowned upon by the union and was called "working the hook."

According to retired journeyman printer Fil Valdez, jeffing survived until the 1960s in the shops throughout the western

**"In the Days That Wuz": "Jeffing" for the only sub.—
and he doesn't care to work**

Fig. 20. Jeffing for a shift of work. Drawn by John T. Nolf for the *Inland Printer*, 1929. Reprinted from the *Inland Printer* with the permission of *American Printer*/Maclean Hunter Publishing Co. All rights reserved.

states where he worked. Valdez apprenticed in what he calls the "handpeg" days when foundry types were in ample supply: "When you have one shift and you had three or four different people wanting it, the chairman decided who was going to work the shift by jeffing, or rolling of the type. He'd throw pieces of type, you know. He'd jiggle them around in his hand. And then they would call out the letter they wanted. If they matched it, why that's who got the shift."[15] Things were reportedly different in the East. In New York City union shops the only way a printer got a particular shift was by exercising his or her seniority rights in that shop. When the office posted a shift or starting time, the person with the least seniority was affected by it, unless a printer with more seniority claimed that job.[16]

It is fairly clear that beer drinking is and always has been a cherished component of chapel life. In London, chapel meetings are still frequently held in pubs,[17] and they are referred to as wet chapels. According to Savage, the nineteenth-century chapel never assembled without the fee for a gallon of porter.[18] One suspects that a large portion of chapel revenue went toward financing such refreshments. It appears that many tricks and games were played to insure the chapel fund was sufficiently full. Remember that one was penalized for throwing water at another. Savage reports: "In hot summer weather, when a man has been desirous of a draught of porter, an instance has been known of his falling down in a pretended fit, and when another in kindness has procured some cold water and sprinkled his face with it, the other has jumped up and accused him of throwing water at him, on which he has had to pay the fine."[19]

Being accused of an offense was not the only circumstance under which one was expected to contribute to chapel funds. Marriage, the birth of a son or daughter, and a visit from the wife were all occasions requiring the journeyman to make payment to the chapel. It was also a recognized custom for any newly engaged journeyman to pay half a crown before becoming a member of the chapel. This initiatory payment was called a "bienvenu" (also spelled "benvenue") or "footing." Benjamin Franklin was excommunicated from a London print shop for refusing to pay his bienvenu. Franklin describes the 1720s print shop where an ale-house boy was kept in constant attendance. Franklin's companion at the press drank, each day, "a pint before breakfast, a pint at breakfast with his bread and cheese, a pint in the afternoon about six o'clock, and another when he had done his day's work. . . ."[20]

Drinking was ritualized in other initiatory rites, such as in the following hazing ordination, described in an eighteenth-century trade journal: "When a Boy is to be bound Apprentice, before he be admitted a Chapellonian, it is necessary for Him to be made a Cuz or a Deacon, in the performance of which there are a great many ceremonies. . . . the Boy kneels, and the Father of the Chapel, after exhorting him to be observant of his Business and not to betray the Secrets of the Workmen, squeezes a Spunge of Strong Beer over his Head and gives him a Title, which is generally that of Duke of some Place of least Reputation near where he lives, or did live before such as Rag Fair, Thieving Lane, Puddle Dock, P-ssing Alley and the like."[21]

Once a year, it was the master printer's duty to provide a feast at his own house and to provide the journeymen with money to spend at the alehouse later the same evening. This annual festivity was known as a waygoose (sometimes spelled wayzgoose). Originally, it was held on St. Bartholomew-Tide[22] (24 August) and it marked the time of year when journeymen printers began to work by candlelight. The waygoose eventually evolved into what we know as the company picnic. The owners of a printing establishment funded an outing into the country and a dinner for its employees. Such an outing is portrayed in Albert Halper's novel *The Foundry.*

In recent times, printing history enthusiasts have been known to revive the waygoose tradition, if in name only. A New Mexican–style waygoose was held in Santa Fe by the Press of the Palace of Governors on 24 August 1985, as part of an exhibit opening.[23] Four years later, the second annual "Iowaygoose" was held in Mason City. People came from throughout Iowa as well as from Illinois and Kansas to watch printing demonstrations, take home printed keepsakes, and participate in lots of trading, selling, and shoptalk.[24]

The Tramp Printer

The folklore of the printer's trade could not be complete without a discussion of the legendary traveling printers, otherwise known as tramps. Writing in 1927 for the Diamond Jubilee celebration of the International Typographical Union, Postmaster General Harry S. New stated, "Neither the cowboy of the West, nor the lumberjack of the North, was more certainly a type of American development than was the itinerant printer of a half century ago. . . ."[25]

At some time in their working lives, many journeymen printers answered the call of the road. During the nineteenth century, workers were in demand at different times and at different places. Early printing societies encouraged tramping as a way of removing workers from their area in slack times; they also sought to ensure that those traveling printers who entered town were skilled craftspeople who would not undermine local wage scales.[26]

By the 1850s, traveling cards were issued to all members of the National Typographical Union (established in 1852). The traveling card ensured geographic mobility by entitling journeymen printers admission to a local without payment of initiation fees or dues, as long as their stay was less than a month. If the printing establishment was experiencing a slow time, the tramps were given food money and the right to sleep in the office for the night. The father of the chapel might allow them to distribute just enough type to pay their way out of town.

The union member's traveling card was an indispensable possession. "I always put a lot of faith in that card," says Amelia Story, now eighty-one, who took to the road back in the 1940s. "If you saw that card, you knew that you were going to get justice."[27]

A fictional scene from *Trampography: Reminiscences of a Rovin' Printer 1913 to 1917,* written under the pseudonym Linafont Brevier, further illustrates what the card came to symbolize for union printers. In this book, a young traveling printer enters a print shop, carrying with him samples of his work in hopes of getting hired. The proprietor is a union man. "Listen kid," he tells him, "we printers who call ourselves printers, never carry samples around with us to show what we can do, or have done. Our card is the only credential we need to prove to prospective employers that we *are* printers."[28]

William Pretzer defines four phases of tramping, the last of which extended from the introduction of the Linotype in the late 1880s into the Great Depression of the 1930s.[29] In 1988, it was still possible to meet and talk with printers who "rode the rails," especially by walking the halls of the Union Printers Home in Colorado Springs. One resident there, who was too young to have tramped himself, spoke of the tradition:

"Sure, ride the rails. In later generations they had cars. And they would get a job just to support themselves. A lot of it was not forced on them, a lot of them liked to travel. They liked the roaming business.

"Oh, I could point people out to you here that probably roamed all over the United States."[30]

Having traveled extensively is often a point of pride. Neil "Angelface" Fuller, who was born in 1890, boasts that he traveled across from New York to the West Coast six times in an automobile, finding work wherever he stopped.[31] Amelia Story, who started working when she was fifteen, in the year 1917, speaks pridefully of the man who first hired her: "My boss and his brother were what they call tramp printers, in their handset days. They traveled all over the United States. He said he believed they worked in every state in the union and never got fired. Neither one of them."[32]

Fil Valdez remembers a tramp who rode the broncos from Texas to the Canadian border. "When he felt like it and he needed some money, he'd put in a shift someplace."

Fil asks me if I have ever heard of the Wandering Jew. I recalled seeing a printed article on the Wandering Jew, in a display case of the home's museum, which pictured an old man with a very long beard.

"He used to go all over. When I was a kid, he came through Raton [New Mexico]. He did a few little jobs. And he used to sell these little books he had written. Little humorous books, jewels of wisdom, as he called them."

"So he was a legendary character?" I ask and Fil nods. "And you *met* him?" One does not usually meet legendary characters.

"Yeah. He'd pick up a shift or two. Then go on.

"Then later on when I went to Arizona, damn if I didn't run into him again. And he recognized me, you know."

"Was he older?"

"Oh yeah, hell, he was forty years older than me. He was an old man already. He came right up to me, says, 'I knew you in Raton, New Mexico.' What a mind, you know?

"And then, I went out to the coast. And damn if he didn't come out over there. I met him at the *Chronicle,* in San Francisco. He says, 'You know,' he says, 'You're just like horse shit; you're all over the place.'

"I told him, 'Well, I'm following your footsteps.'

"Oh, we had a great time. But I like to talk about him because I knew the guy. The Wandering Jew. Yeah, he was quite a legend among the printers."[33]

Tramp printers epitomized the journeymen's values of respectability, reciprocity, and independence.[34] In later years, tramps were a living reminder of the freedom abandoned by the resident workers, who had to abide by systematized rules. It is not surprising that tramps are both romanticized and vilified in narrative. Stories are told of "Old John," a tramp printer of formidable capabilities. His reputed method of quitting a job speaks to what must have been the secret desire of many compositors faced with distributing type. Instead of placing each sort back in its proper space, Old John would "sweep his left hand over the case, with something of a pontifical gesture, while a quarter column of type tumbled hither and yon, as it must. 'Get to your respective places!' he would command the types"[35] and leave, hitting the road.

Tramp printers are associated with an excessive devotion to the bottle. One writer characterized tramps as "journeymen at the bar as well as at the typestand."[36] Another writer, the pseudonymous Linafont Brevier, offered numerous sketches to support this characterization. His *Trampography* is dedicated to the oldtime tramp printers, knights of the road who often rode the "lower case" (without a ticket) all over the United States. Included in the reminiscences is one tramp's situation in Killdeer, North Dakota:

"I really liked the work, and remained somewhat abstemious on one-half of one beer through week days, but Saturday night I would look over my collection of the *best* that North Dakota, being dry, could sell legally—Perona, Vanilla Extract, Jamaica Ginger (Jake) and Webster's Bitters. . . .

"I went to the other printing office to see about a job. 'Sure,' said the proprietor. 'You take over; I'll be gone about five days. When I get back, have the paper ready to print.'

"Just like that. Four pages, seven columns, 13 ems wide, all hand set with the exception of some boiler plate! I got my 'apprentice'—a bottle—and we (the bottle and I) went to work." [37]

The characterization of the tramp printer as boozer holds up in oral tradition. Joe Malady comments:

"Well, the tramp printer is a tradition among printers. He was noted for his drinking capacity. He would sometimes go from one town to another and get a job and work long enough to get money so he could go on a spree."

Upon arriving in town, the tramp reputedly made his way to the first printing office or bar, whichever he ran into first. Joe explains, "The drinking was just part of it. It was part of a conviviality, I suppose from the trade itself. From the fact that these people were all strangers in new towns and there was a social gathering at a bar. So any itinerant worker usually heads for a bar, which substitutes for social clubs or church groups. It has the same connotation; it's a place where you meet people and talk to people."

I cannot tell whether Joe is being sarcastic when he adds, "Yeah, those were the glamorous days—the days of the tramp printer, when printing was glamorous."

Some women took to the road as well. Joe recalls a woman resident at the Printers Home, who had died not too long ago. She was known as "Rambling Rose." He remarks, "She was known all over the country. Her husband was a printer too. Together they traveled East Coast to West Coast. And people know her. People come in [to the Printers Home] from Texas, California, and they know her."[38]

Women travelers had the protection of the ITU General Laws (1885), which provided that "subordinate unions, foremen and chapels shall make no distinction on account of sex in persons holding international traveling cards."[39] Amelia Story traveled alone in the 1940s, looking to practice her trade. She recalls, "I took a traveler. I went to work in Kansas City and from there I went to Chicago." Amelia eventually made her way to Alaska where she went to work on the *Anchorage Daily Times*. Unlike her male colleagues, the first place she headed for upon arriving in town was not a tavern, but the local YWCA. People there would assist her in getting living quarters.

It was the decline in union membership during the late 1960s that triggered the end of the tramp's peregrinations. Joe Malady, who remembers tramps still roaming around ten years before his retirement in 1978, talks about the calculated elimination of the tramp system: "Young people didn't want to join the union. The printing business was getting low and newspapers were closing. And the papers that existed had only enough work for their local people. They didn't want people with traveling cards coming in from outside. So they would get a grant from headquarters to close that particular city from accepting traveling cards. And gradually, more and more cities got on to that. By 1986 about every major city had asked for an exemption from the traveling card."[40]

Typelice and Paper Stretchers: Initiation Pranks

Tramping, jeffing, bienvenus, and waygooses may have gone by the wayside with the passing of hot metal, but there is one occupational tradition that has endured to this day. The initiation prank—the dreaded rite suffered by many a printer's apprentice— is still practiced, despite the transition to cold type. The prank has survived; only the materials have changed.

Imagine a printing house, circa 1940. A favorite prank of the journeymen printers was to send the newly arrived apprentice, otherwise known as the printer's devil, off on an impossible errand. A young apprentice might have been sent to fetch a "paper stretcher" (a nonexistent item) or given a brush and told to sweep away the typelice (also nonexistent).

"Well, that's what they did. Get the kid to chase for a paper stretcher," says Frank Koncel, recalling the composing room at the *Chicago American*.

"Yeah, send him out to look for a paper stretcher," Jim Spurlock chuckles. "There were a lot of jokes like that. They'd send the kid down, he'd go through about six different departments to see where they left the paper stretcher at."

Like every other printer I have talked with, Jim Spurlock has a story about typelice. "They'd take a galley and put a bunch of water in it, see? And the kid would come over and they'd say, 'The typelice is all in this water, but you have to get *real close* to see it.'

"Well, he would get right down," Jim leans over and squints. Suddenly, he claps his hands together. "Whank! And it would splash his face just full of water. It was nothing harmful, it just wet you all over."

Frank giggles and says with a degree of malice in his voice, "We didn't use water. We used the type wash—what we washed the type with, the gas."

"Oh, you mean the Benzine?" I say. "Wouldn't that hurt?" Frank responds by shrugging his shoulders and uttering a skeptical, "Well?"[41]

John Peckham, a longtime employee of the prestigious Meriden-Stinehour Press, tells almost the identical story:

"I had typelice pulled on me. The green kid comes in. One of the oldtimers has untied the string [that held the lines of Linotype slugs together] and poured water over it.

"He called the kid over, 'Did you see these little bugs that attack the type? Come over here.'

"The kid would come see. 'No, you gotta' look really close,' the oldtimer would say.

Fig. 21. The education of the apprentice. Drawn by W. J. Enright for the *Inland Printer,* n.d. Reprinted from the *Inland Printer* with permission of *American Printer*/Maclean Hunter Publishing Co. All rights reserved.

"That happened to me at Princeton."[42]

Before becoming a folklorist, Kenneth S. Goldstein had worked in the printing industry. In the 1950s he held a job as evening production man at a downtown New York City publishing house called Fairchild Publications. He recalls:

"One of the more interesting things I saw done was the first trick played on the new kid working in the typography office. He would be sent out to get a pair of parallel lines. They would tell him where to start and then say, 'If he doesn't have it, they'll tell you where to get it.'

"He would go to whoever he was referred to and they would say, 'I lent it to Harry last week. I don't have it.' He would get ahold of Harry who would say, 'I gave it to Tom.' Tom would say, 'I think it is up with the Art Production Department,' and he would come up to *me*.

"I would say, 'Well, I put it in an envelope last week and sent it down to Tom so he should have it unless it's gone lost.'

"He'd go back to Tom. They would start him down again and after awhile he'd realize. Some kids were thick in the noggin! It might take only four or five guys, but sometimes it would be eight or nine guys! Eventually he would realize that he was being had.

"And then they would usually take him down to the bar, which was near Fairchild Publications, and have a drink with him. They'd all laugh about it. But the kid would be on his guard for about a week or two."

Goldstein recalls that this prank was specifically thought of as the typographer's joke. "It was all done in good humor. I've never seen anybody really get mad over it, especially since it was followed up afterwards with discovery by the kid. They would discuss it over a drink, 'Oh, now he's a pro. Now he's a *real* typographer. Next time we have a new kid coming in, we're going to send him over to *you* to get something.'"[43]

These initiation pranks afforded the old hands a good laugh at the greenhorn's expense. Though the bienvenu is no longer collected, there is still a price to be paid for membership. The fool's errand is commonplace in occupational life; stories abound from the already initiated among pro football players, mechanics (a left-handed monkey wrench), road builders (a rock stretcher), hunters (a snipe), and flight attendants.

Such pranks are old tricks and certainly not restricted to the workplace. All one has to do is successfully send a friend to the shelf by asking, "Did you know the word gullible is not in the dictionary?" The word exists, but he or she is still made to feel a fool for looking.

A modern-day example of a printer's initiation prank comes from a university student who had spent a summer working at a typesetting firm in the Meadowlands of New Jersey. She recalled that on her first day she was asked to go down to the basement and bring up a bucket of halftone dots. To begin with, the building had no basement. Secondly, halftone dots are no more fetchable than the black and white lines on your television screen.[44] By substituting halftone dots for typelice, the young woman's experience can be seen as the same prank adapted to the contemporary technology at hand. Whether a greenhorn is sent after typelice, moiré patterns, or halftone dots, the educational function of the prank is apparent. Items are chosen that necessitate meaningful explanation of a fairly sophisticated technology. The novice is introduced simultaneously to technical and social customs of the trade.

The continuity of a prank based on knowing your terms is no coincidence. The importance of mastering terminology can never be overemphasized for someone learning the trade. This was made clear to me during my eleven-month stint as an assistant to Carl Gross, design and production manager of a university press. From the very first day, he insisted on the correct usage of terminology. Like the proper tool for the job, there was one and only one way to say things. What at first struck me as unyielding rigidity, later made good economic sense. One slipup in name or number could lose hundreds of dollars and precious time.

Next to mastering terminology, nothing beats getting your

hands dirty. Carl summed it up this way: "The ideal thing is to set type by hand. All your terminology, or at least 80 percent used today, comes from hot metal. You can give someone a definition of a term but it's not the same thing as sitting down at a Linotype machine and learning the meaning of 'squirt' by having the hot metal get all over you. There's no better way to understand the justification of a line of type than to see the space bands pushing up, squeezing the line out." [45]

Swifts, Shoemakers, and Smooth Operators

Aside from the inherent interest for folklorists of printers' verbal lore as expressive communication, there is the occupation-specific value placed on trade and technical terminology to consider. Informants and textbooks repeatedly stress that much of current practice and terminology derives from hot-metal technology. The importance of understanding this phase in the history of printing seems universal among practitioners. Longstanding rules and conventions of hot-metal typography, standards to which the best printers have always adhered, grew out of the built-in limitations of working with materials such as metal and wood. In today's world of computerized typesetting, these limitations are virtually eliminated, as are the majority of manual skills once required of the hot-metal compositor—unless, of course, the opportunity arises for a printer to reinforce didactically the limitations, as in the following story. The tangibility and inflexibility of hot-metal composition were made memorably clear to editor Karen Gaines, who remembers a day from her high school print shop (circa 1949):

"We had this teacher, Mr. Scardino. We worked on the Linotype setting high school weeklies. He'd set your name and then fling the hot slug into your hands. Like a hot potato, you'd throw it up in the air.

"'That's to teach you that type's not rubber. Don't tell me to squeeze one more line of type into this page!'" [46]

"In the Days That Wuz"—The Usual Happening
Cartoon by John T. Nolf, Printer-Artist

Fig. 22. Out of sorts. Drawn by John T. Nolf for the *Inland Printer*, January 1927. Reprinted from the *Inland Printer* with permission of *American Printer/* Maclean Hunter Publishing Co.

The technical and trade terms shared by those in the printing industry are plentiful. Some terms have entered the mainstream and become a part of our everyday speech. For example, the phrase "out of sorts" derives from the printer's term for individual pieces of type including those bought individually to supplement a font. A font is a family of type in one single size and style. The quantity of each letter varies with frequency of use. Hence, a font will have more *A*'s than *X*'s. Even so, a particular job might call for even more *A*'s, in which case the printer could supplement his font by buying what he called "sorts." If he came up short, he was literally out of sorts, not to mention at his wits' end.

Most terms, however, do not circulate outside the industry. The preface of Carl P. Rollins's *Off the Dead Bank* opens with the following truism: "To a printer the title of this book needs no explanation."[47] Fortunately, for those not versed in the black art, Rollins goes on to explain "the dead bank" as the surface on which a form of type was placed after being printed.

Attention to language used on the job is revealing; terms tell us something about how printers view and value their work. It is not unusual to find tools of the trade envisioned anthropomorphically by their users. The curves of a violin are those of a woman's body; its "voice" "sings" like no other instrument's. Consider the nomenclature of type (see fig. 23), the parts and dimensions of this physical object made of metal. From "head" to "foot" one encounters a "body," "face," "beard," "hairline," "shoulder," "belly," and "feet."

Lest the object go unclothed it is "dressed." "Dressing" or "kerning" type refers to the process of moving two letters closer together to make a better visual fit. In hand-set type, the process involved mortising, i.e., cutting away the shoulder of one type so that it would nest together with the adjacent type.

In the late seventeenth century, dressing entailed a final inspection, both in the production of metal type and in its use in composition. The letter dresser of the typefoundry inspected the type and scraped its surfaces to rid the type of any burrs to insure uniformity of body.[48] To "dress" a chase or a form meant to fit the pages with spacing material known as "furniture" to create the proper margins when the form was printed. Describing the latter process, Moxon uses language that imparts a human vulnerability to the compositor's tools and materials: ". . . both his *Page* and *Notes* stand safer, being clothed with the *Furniture*, than they do when they stand Naked in the *Galley*."[49]

The basic meaning of dressing—quality control—has re-

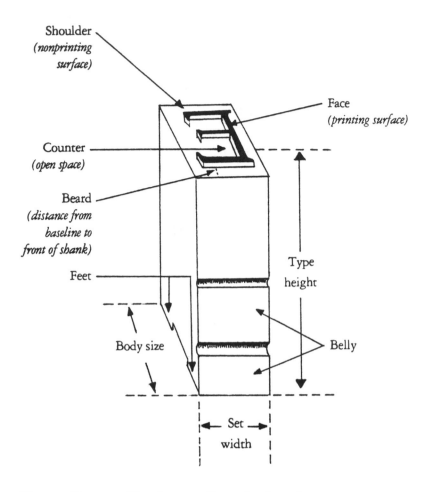

Fig. 23. Diagram of foundry type. Drawn by the author.

mained the same over three centuries. What once was a high-ranking position in the typefoundry, that of letter dresser, became an assumed responsibility of the hand compositor.

Ed Jacob talks about the dressing of type:

"At Curtis, you had to dress the type. If you had the word 'water'. . . ." Ed writes out the word in roman capitals, illustrating the excessive space that would naturally occur between the slope of the *W* and that of the *A* due to the shoulder of the respective types.

". . . all right, if you set it like that [without dressing] you'd get a warning. The next time, you got fired because what they would do is mortise *this* letter [the *W*] and mortise *this* letter [*A*] so that the *A* was tucked in next to the *W* without all that space in between. That's dressing. It was understood it had to be done. No, you didn't ask.

"Today they'll call it kerning. They'll say 'kerning.' But years ago, in a good place, they didn't say anything. You did it."

The majority of employer expectations regarding quality work may have been left unenunciated, but Ed remembers a particularly unreasonable boss:

"This one turkey, Delmare Smith, was a real son of a bitch. No matter what you did, he had to do something to it. *Even* if he said, 'copper more, copper less,' he *had* to do it. He'd never admit that you did it right the first time.

"So, in the *Saturday Evening Post* they would set the headings in 48 point [type]. You had to dress it. 'Course *he* would dress it. 'Dress it again,' he'd tell you. Then he okays it.

"Well, this was all foundry type. It was distributed back in the case. So we were young turks at the time, we thought we'd twick his nose. We saved this title because it was a three-issue series. And we put it back in next month. And what he'd said was perfect, sure as hell he'd 'copper in, copper out.'"

"And you could call him on it?" I ask Ed.

"Nah, Christ, not him."

We both laugh.

"Ho, never." [50]

The term "dressing" is not restricted to the printing trade. It was used by railroad workers as well. Cornelius Wright, Jr., worked as a track foreman at US Steel in Birmingham, Alabama, before the mechanization of track labor. He talks about dressing the gravel bed that the ties lay on so the water would drain away from the track.

"There wasn't a pebble out of place. You took your shovel and you *dressed* it and you patted it and you smoothed it out. It was a thing of art almost. When you looked down the track, you could see the beauty. You didn't see all the weeds."[51]

Anthropomorphism extends beyond the nomenclature and handling of type. The printer's language of evaluation tends toward active terminology. In order to talk critically about a page of printed text, one specifies "running feet," "head margins," "bastard titles," "widows" and "orphans," "monks" and "friars." A book has a "spine," "headbands," and "footbands."

If not directly anthropomorphic, terms are generally animate. A faulty page is plagued with "rivers" of white space caused by loose word-spacing in successive lines of type. Rivers are more apt to crop up when one is setting justified lines of type, i.e., lines of even length (see fig. 24). Rivers are no more acceptable today than they were in the late seventeenth century. Moxon notes, "These wide *Whites* are by *Compositors* (in way of Scandal) call'd *Pigion-holes,* and are not accounted good Workmanship. . . ."[52]

An illustration or photograph that extends to the trim edge is called a bleed. Type is matter; during its composition it is referred to as "type matter." Broken or battered type is thrown into the "hellbox" and melted down.

On a weekly, a story that doesn't get in is "overmatter." If the editor wants to ask about any obligations from the preceding week he or she will say, "Is there anything still alive?"[53] Once a book is printed and bound the proof is returned to the publisher marked "foul matter" or "dead matter"—proof that the type is envisioned as alive and active only through one's intervention with it.

In addition to the operational and evaluative terms for the products of work, there are those for the workman. A "shoemaker" is a "real slop artist." Why shoemaker? I asked Bert Powers. "'Cause they were *shoemakers*" [i.e., not printers]. The habit of invoking other trades to imply poor craftsmanship appears to be a custom of some duration. In Pietro Di Donato's novel *Christ in Concrete,* the term comes up when a gathering of bricklayers are

COLLEGES ARE REUNITING THE
HUMANITIES AND THE SCIENCES

C. P. Snow, the British scientist and novelist, sounded the alarm in the 1950s about the dangers of two cultures: "Literary intellectuals at one pole, at the other scientists." Since then, microchips, satellites and nuclear power have become realities that define everyday life; yet many supposedly well-educated people do not understand how they work. Despite the growing use of computers in classrooms, American universities are still graduating millions of technological illiterates.

What Snow called a "gulf of mutual incomprehension" yawns ever wider, according to Stanford Engineering Professor James Adams, who describes the problem as a conflict between the "techs" (engineers and scientists) and the "fuzzies" (liberal arts student): "The techs are considered by the fuzzies to be nerds. The techs, in turn, consider the fuzzies as only marginal at reaching logical conclusions, probably unable to keep their bicycles in operation and completely unable to support themselves after graduation."

In 1980 a survey funded by the National Science Foundation of 215 institutions concluded that the average humanities major spent only about 7% of his college education studying science. Hence the Alfred P. Sloan Foundation is making grants of more than $3 million to 32 of the nation's top liberal arts colleges in order to introduce the reasoning methods used in applied mathematics and the development of technology into today's liberal arts curriculum. Sloan will provide $250,000 each to ten colleges, including Williams, Mount Holyoke and Wellesly, and $25,000 to others, such as Dartmouth and Bowdoin, to attack the deficiencies of their curriculums.

(quoted from Time, December 6, 1982, p. 61).

Fig. 24. Example of a "river" of white space caused by poor typesetting.

discussing the taking on of a new apprentice by an elder named Nazone, who is known more for his kindness than his skill as a bricklayer: "Nazone as a bricklayer may be a shoemaker, but he has a warm little heart beating under his arm."[54]

The blacksmith also served as a personification of shoddy workmanship. "Notwithstanding all that has been written and said about the spread and increase of amateurism and *blacksmithing* [emphasis added] in the printing trade, it cannot be denied that, as a whole, the jobwork of the present time is vastly superior to anything accomplished . . . in the past."[55]

Here is a mid-nineteenth-century use of the term by a newly hired compositor: ". . . [he] asked if I considered myself a first-class book compositor. He said they were very particular about spacing, etc. He offered to let me have a fair trial, and then he

Fig. 25. Atlanta-area newspaper composing room, undated. Used with permission of the Southern Labor Archives, Georgia State University.

could tell what I could do. If I came in Monday I might try and see what I could do. Just as likely as not I shall turn out a 'blacksmith.'"[56]

Ed Jacob used the term "shoemaker" to refer to newspaper compositors. "They couldn't come to our place and work. The newspaper is a different world. These people from the junk shops, cellar shops—they wouldn't last at all."

"They wouldn't learn?" I ask.

"Nah. You could almost tell in a couple of hours. We could see it. The foreman could tell by us laughing, that he has a real shoemaker on his hands. Right? He might give him the whole day or he'd tell him to get out at lunch.

"Consequently, if the shop was large, somehow, somebody would be able to get a line on you. If no one knew you and you said, 'Well, I worked at Company X,' somebody in that crowd knows somebody at Company X. And they'd say, 'Is Maggie a shoemaker?' And if they say, 'Yeah,' you wouldn't even start."[57]

Compare Ed's story to this fictionalized scene from Brevier's *Trampography:* "If you are just an ordinary printer, don't take off your coat," said the skipper, "because I'll know in the first hour. But if you are a better than ordinary printer, you'll have a steady job."[58]

The antithesis of a shoemaker is a "swift," someone who can set type *very* accurately and *very* fast. The term dates back to the nineteenth century, before the invention and widespread acceptance of linecasting machines. One writer remarked, "Every printer will remember the youthful days when his ambition was to set the biggest string[59] on the paper, and hope was high in his breast that he might be considered a 'swift.'"[60]

The printer, holding a composing stick in the left hand, picked up types from individual compartments and placed them upside down and backward into the stick. How swiftly and efficiently one went through the motions was a factor, especially among newspaper printers who were used to setting copy under the constant pressure of the next edition. Money was also an incentive to work swiftly, for in some shops printers were paid by the em, or piece, instead of by the hour. With speed, dexterity, and accuracy at a premium, it is no wonder that typesetting contests were commonplace.

I found a faded photograph of one of these competitions (fig. 26) squirreled away in an oak cabinet in an administrative office of the Union Printers Home. A photograph taken from a slightly different angle, but clearly on the same day, appeared in the pages of the *Inland Printer* with the following caption: "'Swifts' of Other Days Settle Mastership Claims at the Case."[61] The typesetting contest was staged by superintendent Joe S. Daley who explained that he had grown tired of the "boasting lies some of the residents had been telling about their prowess in 'handset days.'"[62] Type cases were set up on the front lawn of the home, and James M. Lynch, then president of the International Typographical Union, served as

Fig. 26. Swifts settle claims of prowess in old-fashioned typesetting contest on the lawn of the Union Printers Home, circa 1925.

the referee. The prize went to sixty-three-year-old Joe Price for setting five hundred ems in pica in twenty minutes—no small feat.

Once the Linotype machine had caught on, "swift" was replaced by a new phrase, "hang the elevator," which derived from the limitations of the Linotype machine. The elevator was one of many parts involved in the assembly of matrices and spaces. For an operator to outrun, or outfinger, the machine was something worth boasting about.

Frank Koncel remembers one individual in particular: "Ollie Chamberlain. Boy, he could *hang the elevator* setting agate [a small point size used in newspaper composition]."

"He could do what?" I ask.

"Hang the elevator. He aced it."

Jim Spurlock explains. "That's when you're running the machine as fast as it will run." Frank modifies Jim's explanation. "He would run the machine *faster* than it ran. He was damn good."

"The elevator would be waiting for the line in front to clear before it could go over to the next one."[63]

The phrase is recalled by fifty-eight-year-old Hugh Tims who, for the last fifteen years, has handled all the tricky formatting problems at the computer typesetting company where he works. Tims is one of those fortunate printers who is equally adept in the new technology as he was in the old. Having apprenticed in a small country print shop in east Texas, Tims went on to work at the *Atlanta Journal Constitution* as a Linotype operator. "We would run it so fast till it *hung*. Then we'd drape a handkerchief over the keyboard and wait." He adds that Linotype operators who could run the machine like this were called "smooth operators."[64]

Collective values and standards concerning quality, speed, and accuracy are inherent in the language used by the printer. One begins to sense what constitutes the printer's "canon of technique," a concept developed by Robert McCarl to describe "the traditionally-based criteria used to judge technical competence in work culture."[65] The canon is not a fixed set of rules but the collective ability and performance that one applies in the daily course of one's work.

Ed Jacob recalled a conversation with a fellow he had worked with for years. This man mentioned to Ed that Otto had died. Ed had responded with a small chuckle, "Oh, Otto, the piano player." In response to my perplexed look he told the following story.

To better visualize what Ed is talking about let me explain that pages of composed type are arranged in a rectangular frame, called a chase, in preparation for printing. The pages are surrounded by "furniture" and tightened with wedges, known as "quoins." This assemblage of parts is called a "form."

In order to transport a form to the bed of the press, the compositor must lock it up. Ed explains: "Okay, when you lock up a form you take the key and put it underneath here. And you take your fist and *pound* that damn thing."

Ed slams his fist down on the lunch table.

"You'd pound on it. And if something would drop, you had to open it up because somewhere, something was binding; it wasn't letting it lock up properly.

"Okay, well, if you're doing your job right, you really took a whack at this thing—you didn't damage anything—to see if it was tight. First of all, so it didn't fall out. Second place, if it *was* binding it meant something would come out crooked, okay?

"Well, Otto was not the greatest craftsman. And instead of hitting this thing, he'd go. . . ." Ed demonstrates by lightly running his fingers up and down the table top.

"'Kay? So these were piano players, okay? The piano player. See, he would tickle it. Nothing would ever fall. And then we'd come up, you know. They would hang the sheets on a hook. They'd have a hook for 'finished' and a hook 'to do.' And you'd go over there and you'd see Otto's job next—you'd take a walk over to the fountain! You'd figure, 'Oh Christ,' you know, 'I gotta open this thing up because *he* never checked it.' So we would try to avoid his work, see." [66]

Ed's story clarified the term "piano player." It also explicated Ed's relationship to a canon of technique—communally defined knowledge about materials, technique in manipulating them, and some of the communicative avenues of judging competence or lack of it on the job.

Printing plants themselves were subject to critical evaluation. *What* the plant printed determined the quantity, speed, and quality of workmanship. Ed Jacob distinguishes among job printers (business cards, posting bills, tickets), commercial printers, and book printers: "A job shop would do anything. Commercial generally meant better quality or book [work]. But then you had your book shops. That was tops. Cellar shop—that was real garbage. Quick and dirty printing. Hatchet work." [67]

As printing technology evolves, so must occupational language. The use of the word "leading" has already been mentioned. Another example of the shift away from literal meaning is the use of the terms "upper case" and "lower case." In the composing room

"In the Days That Wuz"—On the Outside

Fig. 27. The piano player. Drawn by John T. Nolf for the *Inland Printer*,
1928. Reprinted from the *Inland Printer* with permission of *American Printer/
Maclean Hunter Publishing Co. All rights reserved.

of the printer's shop, foundry type was stored in shallow wooden
cases.[68] The top half of the case was called the "upper case" and it
held the capital letters; the bottom half, or "lower case," held the
minuscule letters.[69] In today's parlance, the phrase "upper and
lower case," or its abbreviation, U/lc, is directive rather than nom-
inative, indicating to the typesetter a specific use of type, rather
than a physical location of its storage.

**Upper
Case**

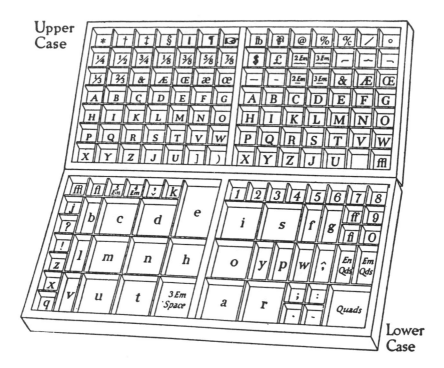

**Lower
Case**

Fig. 28 The news typecase. From Daniel B. Updike, *Printing Types, Their
History, Forms, and Use,* vol. 1 (1937; reprint New York: Dover Publications,
1980), p. 21.

"Galleys" no longer mean the brass or wooden trays that held
lines of composed type; they are the paper proofs of those lines,
printed. In a modern-day typesetting firm there are no metal galleys because there is no metal type to go in them. The name remains because the width and length of the original galley trays
became the standardized length of galley proofs we use today.

In printer's terms, "30" means the end. The derivation of this
term comes from hot-metal practice as well. A 30-point slug, cast
by the Linotype machine, measuring approximately 7/16 inches in
height, was used at the bottom of the galley to indicate the end of
a take. The symbol was also commonly used by reporters on ending their stories. The only time one would actually see "30" in

print was when a newspaper folded and it ran its last issue. It is not surprising that an article by ITU vice president Allen J. Heritage, discussing the union's impending merger with the CWA, was headlined "30."[70] For anyone who has ever worked in hot metal, the symbol "30" is coterminous with "the end." But for that increasing majority of typesetters raised in a cold-type environment, "30" is just a number.

Some hot-metal terms survive, like "leading," having been appropriated for new techniques. Others, like "30," get lost altogether because their relative functions have been lost.

For the journeyman printer working in a hot-metal composing room, the tangibility and built-in limitations of his materials defined the controlled freedom under which all true craftsmen work. The compositor practiced a marketable skill held by few, which is described in some detail below.

Both hand composition and linecasting machine composition are processes that involve the physical building up of component parts. These parts are assembled to make up the form, which must be capable of being lifted while pressure is applied to all four sides, without any of the component parts falling out. The individual lines of type that make up the pages of the form must be of uniform length. The process of varying interword spacing to achieve this uniform length is called "justification" and it requires visual judgment and manual skill.

In hand composition, a practice dating back to the fifteenth century, foundry type is picked out and placed in a composing stick.[71] A printer must learn to read and compose type upside down and backwards. (See fig. 29.)

Manufacturers of composing sticks competed for the printer's loyalty, as this 1930s advertisement copy shows: "A Rouse stick, in the hand of the present-day journeyman, identifies him as a printer of ability . . . no less definitely than his Union Card!"

After the compositor has filled his stick with several lines of text, he transfers them to a galley where type matter, illustration material, and furniture (the blocks of wood or metal spacing material used to hold type matter in position) are combined in an

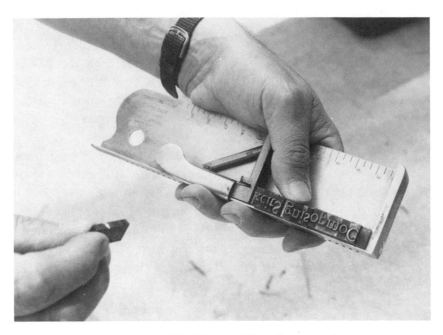

Fig. 29. Rouse composing stick with type. Photo by the author.

aesthetic arrangement to make up a page. This work involves a combination of manual dexterity, physical strength, patience, and visual judgment—what is known as "an eye." Once pages are made up, they are secured and laid in position on an imposing stone, a flat, smooth-surfaced work table. Here, books are created.

Compositors with this specialized skill earn the title of "stonehand" or "stoneman." Bob Culp observed, "A stoneman is a compositor, but not every compositor is a stoneman. That's *heavy* work. I spent the extra year as an apprentice to learn stonework." [72] Acquiring all the skills in composition work gave Bob a sense of pride as well as a degree of job security. "Now I'm going to make a statement: I was laid off many times but I never lost a day of work."

Four months later, Bob reiterated, "Five years was the standard apprenticeship. I spent the extra year and learned every aspect

Fig. 30. Stonework being done by Sarge Bare of Heritage Printers, 1986. Photo by the author.

of composing. I like variety. As they say, 'last man hired, first man fired'; that's why when I was laid off, I never missed a day of work. When they let go a stoneman or a Linotype operator, I could claim that job."

A colleague of Bob's at Chilton, Tony Donaghy, put this versatility in financial terms. "Where the money was, that's where I was. Stonehands got *premium* money."

Bob Culp mentioned that Tony Donaghy had moved out to the Union Printers Home, so I look for him when I make a trip to Colorado Springs.

On my first day at the home, I find my way to the administrative offices. There I meet Mr. Fifield, whose background is hospital administration, not printing. Indeed, he is the home's first chief administrator not to come from a printing background, which troubles a good many residents. I mention to Fifield that some of the printers I've talked with back east know some of the residents in the home. Fifield asks me who, for instance. The first name that comes to mind is Tony Donaghy, the stonehand.

"Tony Donaghy," I say.

Fifield answers, with some satisfaction, "Well, there he is, right behind you." I turn around to see a man with wispy hair, in pajamas and robe, who has wheeled himself into the office to work out some Medicare business. He has fallen recently and smashed a kneecap. Fifield asks him if he would be willing to talk with me. "Sure," he answers, "I've got nothing to do. Twenty-four hours a day."

Four days later and Tony Donaghy has taken another fall. This time he breaks his hip. He is moved from the Printers Home to St. Francis Hospital, six blocks away. I telephone patient information to find out how Tony is doing. They tell me he is recovering in room 433, bed 1. I ring the nurses' station and they connect me to Tony's phone.

"Who is this?"

"Maggie, from the Printers Home. I met you in the front office on Monday."

He remembers and says yes, he would like a visitor.

"What did you say your name was?"

"Maggie."

"Oh. A nice Irish name." I decide to leave it at that.

The walk to the hospital takes a good twenty minutes. The city blocks seem incredibly long to an easterner. Sidewalks and parking lots are still covered with the preceding day's snowfall and remnants of Sunday night's ice storm.

At the nurses' station I am told that Tony Donaghy was operated on the previous day for hip-pin surgery, but that he will be allowed to leave in two days. I find the room, knock, and introduce myself. He is seated out of bed in a wheelchair, connected with intravenous tubes to bottles and drains. The pastel green of the hospital gown and the stubble on his unshaven face make him look weak and weary, until he smiles, which he does a good deal during the course of my visit.

He tells me that he is from Sharon Hill, "the end of the line past Upper Darby." Having lived in West Philadelphia, I can picture the stable working-class neighborhood with its rowhouses and trolley lines. When I ask him if anyone else in his family was in the printing business, he laughs.

"They're *all* printers. I'll start off with my father. He comes home to me one day and says, 'I've got a job for you at Chilton. Who the hell's gonna' pay for my new car?'

"My brother worked at Lanston Monotype Company. My father was a printer. My father-in-law was the boss of Chilton. And my grandfather was a type designer."

"Did any of your children go into printing?"

"Printing was all over with by the time my kids got going."

Tony Donaghy is seventy-eight years old and has been at the home since October 1982. When I ask him which union locals some of the other residents of the home are from he says, "You don't say where you're from unless you're bragging.

"When I came here [UPH] we had about four to five there from work." He raises his eyebrows, opening his eyes wide, and smiles. "Chilly Thompson, a proofreader, Ed Howard, Amele Linnegan."

"Did you know a man named Herman Tuchinsky?" I ask him.

"I sure did. And Dan Burns, he was one of our top men."

"What about Bob Campbell?" I ask, remembering Bob Culp's fond memories of these men.

"Yeah, Bob Campbell was another stonehand. They were the ones that knew more about the business than anyone else. When it goes to the stone, it's gotta be pretty near perfect."

The printing business was good to Tony Donaghy. Like many other printers of his generation, the sense of prestige derived from his occupational identity is an ongoing source of tremendous pride.[73] "The money was good. Yeah, you weren't bashful when you said you were a printer."[74]

Notes

1. Joe Malady, member of Atlantic City Local No. 377, tape-recorded interview, 2 February 1988.

2. Tony Donaghy, visit in his room at St. Francis Hospital where he was recovering from a broken hip, Colorado Springs, 4 February 1988. Tony remembered the incident. "Dan's brother was hit by a trolley car. The Island Road trolley near the airport. Well, he wasn't getting the right treatment in the public hospital. So I went in and blew my top."

3. Moxon, *Mechanick Exercises*, 323.

4. See Thompson, "Customs of the Chapel," 330.

5. *The Pied Printer's Primrose Path: A Typographical Nonsense Book* (Stamford, Ct.: Overbrook Press, 1940), [10].

6. In this case "blankets" refer to the pressman's sheets of softer paper that lay underneath the top tympan-sheet. The "tympan" is the paper packing that is placed between the impression surface of a press and the paper to be printed. On modern-day offset lithography presses, the printing of images directly onto paper is avoided. Instead, the inked image is transferred, or "offset," onto a smooth rubber blanket, which in turn transfers the image onto an impression cylinder carrying the paper.

7. William Savage, *A Dictionary of the Art of Printing* (1841, reprint, New York: Burt Franklin, 1967), 164–68.

8. Moxon, *Mechanick Exercises*, 324.

9. Savage, *Art of Printing*, 167.

10. Moxon, *Mechanick Exercises*, 326.

11. "Nicks" are actually curved grooves cut in one side of the metal type. The number and placement of nicks will vary according to the size and style of the typeface being used. See fig. 23.

12. Moxon, *Mechanick Exercises*, 325.

13. George Bayer, "Jeffing," *American Notes and Queries* 6 (1946): 14.

14. John Southward, *A Dictionary of Typography and Its Accessory Arts* (London, 1871), quoted in Thompson, "Customs of the Chapel," 337.

15. Fil Valdez, Albuquerque No. 304, tape-recorded interview in his room at the Union Printers Home in Colorado Springs, 5 February 1988.

16. Carl Schlesinger, personal communication, February 1990.

17. Cockburn, *Brothers*, 18 and 169.

18. Savage, *Art of Printing*, 166.

19. Ibid.

20. Quoted in A. E. Musson, *The Typographical Association: Origins and History up to 1949* (London: Oxford University Press, 1954), 12.

21. *The Country Journal or the Craftsman*, 24 May 1740, quoted by Cockburn, *Brothers*, 17.

22. According to one book of calendric custom, this was the day on which the famous London Fair was held, from the twelfth to the mid-nineteenth century; see Leslie Dunkling, *A Dictionary of Days* (New York: Facts on File, 1988), 9.

23. See the American Printing History Association *APHA Letter* 65, no. 3 (1985): 3.

24. Reported in *The Printer* 4, no. 7 (September 1989): 8.

25. Harry S. New, "Impressions," *Diamond Jubilee 1852–1927* (Indianapolis: International Typographical Union, 1927).

26. See William S. Pretzer's excellent article on tramp printers in America, "Tramp Printers: Craft Culture, Trade Unions, and Technology," *Printing History* 6, no. 2 (1984): 3–16.

27. Amelia Story, tape-recorded interview in her room at the Union Printers Home, 2 February 1988.

28. Linafont Brevier (pseudonym), *Trampography: Reminiscences of a Rovin' Printer 1913 to 1917* (Glendale: n.p., 1954).

29. Pretzer, "Tramp Printers," passim.

30. Joe Malady, tape-recorded interview, 2 February 1988.

31. Neil Fuller was the unofficial historian of the Union Printers Home until his death in September 1988.

32. Amelia Story, tape-recorded interview, 2 February 1988.

33. Fil Valdez, tape-recorded interview, 5 February 1988.

34. Pretzer, "Tramp Printers," 3.

35. Lampman, *The Tramp Printer*, 50.

36. Ibid., 6.

37. Brevier, *Trampography*, 63.

38. Joe Malady, tape-recorded conversation in the lobby of the Union Printers Home, 2 February 1987.

39. Avery, *Saga ITU Oldtimers*, 9.

40. Malady, tape-recorded interview, 2 February 1988.

41. Jim Spurlock and Frank Koncel, tape-recorded interview, 2 February 1988.

42. John Peckham, interview in Meriden, Connecticut, 21 February 1986.

43. Kenneth S. Goldstein, tape-recorded conversation, 2 November 1984.

44. Halftone dots are visible upon close inspection of a newspaper photograph. In order for a glossy original to be reproduced, a screen is used which converts the image into a pattern of dots of varying size. The reproduced photograph, no longer of continuous tone, is called a halftone.

45. Carl Gross, University of Pennsylvania Press, interview, 2 November 1983.

46. Karen Gaines, Editor, *Almanac*, interview, 5 October 1984.

47. Carl P. Rollins, *Off the Dead Bank: Addresses, Reviews, and Verses,* Typophiles Chap Books 19 (New York: The Typophiles, 1949).

48. Moxon, *Mechanick Exercises,* 184.

49. Ibid., 218.

50. Ed Jacob, tape-recorded interview, 30 November 1983.

51. Cornelius Wright, Jr., retired track foreman, tape-recorded interview at his office in Birmingham, 14 October 1988.

52. Moxon, *Mechanick Exercises,* 207.

53. Karen Gaines, interview, 5 October 1984.

54. See Pietro Di Donato, *Christ in Concrete* (New York: Bobbs-Merrill, 1939), 94.

55. Alfred Pye, "Progress in Letterpress Printing," *Inland Printer* (December 1888).

56. "Diary of an Old Printer, The Intimate Experiences of a Composing-room Worker at Harper's in New York Half a Century Ago," [1871], *The American Printer* 70, no. 5 (5 March 1920).

57. Ed Jacob, tape-recorded interview, 30 November 1983.

58. Brevier, *Trampography,* 55.

59. The "biggest string" refers to the way a printer's piecework was accounted for. During the 1800s and early 1900s a printer's daily output of type was measured with a strand of string, which was then measured against a ruler. The length of string therefore indicated how many inches or ems of type were set and what pay was due the printer.

60. Alex Duguid, "Practical Working of Composing Machines," *Inland Printer* (January 1895), from Maurice Annenberg, *A Typographic Journey through the Inland Printer* (Baltimore: Maran Press), 491.

61. *Inland Printer* 75, no. 5 (August 1925): 793.

62. Ibid.

63. Jim Spurlock and Frank Koncel, tape-recorded interview, 2 February 1988.

64. Hugh Tims, conversation at Graphic Composition, Inc., Athens, Georgia, 9 March 1988.

65. Robert McCarl, "You've Come a Long Way and Now This Is Your Retirement: An Analysis of Performance in Fire Fighting Culture," *Journal of American Folklore* 97, no. 386 (1984): 419 n. 3.

66. Ed Jacob, tape-recorded interview, 30 November 1983.

67. Ibid.

68. These printers' cases have been drafted into service in new contexts. One finds them for sale in antique shops and hung on living room walls where they are used to display miniatures and other collectibles.

69. This is true of the news cases which were more common before the general introduction of typesetting machines. The news case was displaced in

popularity by the more convenient and compact California Job Case. The layout of the latter combines both the caps and the lowercase letters in one case.

70. Article in the last issue of *Typographical Journal* (December 1986): 5.

Another version of the origination of "30" is that it was used by railroad telegraphers to indicate they were shutting down for the night. Some say it had to do with a "Rule 30," which spelled out a temporary shutting of telegraph operations. Carl Schlesinger, personal communication, February 1990.

71. A description of the composing stick, its use and care, is covered in the ITU correspondence course textbook, *Lessons in Printing: Elements of Composition* (Indianapolis: International Typographical Union, 1959), 140, 174–76. For an entertaining historical account of the composing stick as tool see Martin R. Speckter, *Disquisition on the Composing Stick* (New York: The Typophiles, 1971).

72. Bob Culp, told to me during work, 21 June 1984.

73. According to the 1947 Roper study cited in Blauner, printing ranked first in positive job identification out of all industrial workers surveyed; see Blauner, *Alienation and Freedom,* 47.

74. Tony Donaghy, interview at St. Francis Hospital, Colorado Springs, 4 February 1988.

4

The Hot-Metal Process

Metal Typecasting Machines

Technically, hand-set composition is not considered hot metal, since it involves no molten lead. "Hot metal" is the term used to describe type composition done with casting machines such as the Linotype and Monotype. In the former, an "operator" sits at a keyboard and selects character matrices which are mechanically assembled into justified lines of text. Molten metal alloy, hence the term "hot metal," is pumped against the character side of these matrices, which are subsequently redistributed to their proper home in the magazine.[1]

In the Monotype system, keyboarding and casting operations are separated. Striking a key perforates a roll of paper tape (similar to a player piano roll), which is then fed to a casting machine. Like their names suggest, the Linotype casts a line of type (called a slug) while the Monotype casts individual type characters.

When the technology developed in the 1930s to send impulses over telegraph and telephone wires, type could be keyboarded in one location on a teletypesetting keyboard (TTS) and cast at another. These tape-controlled linecasting machines, with their basic typewriter-lay keyboards, were a threat to the craft nature of the composing room. The division of labor between keyboarding and typecasting separated the intellective aspects of work from the physical execution of work. Computer-based technology was applied to the TTS in the 1960s. Semiskilled workers could type unfinished (i.e., unjustified) tape and feed it to a computer

Fig. 31. Linotype operator seated at original "Blower" model, circa 1886–91. From the *Inland Printer*, 1899. Reprinted from the *Inland Printer* with permission of *American Printer*/Maclean Hunter Publishing Co. All rights reserved.

for processing. The skilled compositor could be bypassed altogether.[2]

From the turn of the century up until the mid-1970s, most text composition was produced with the aid of linecasting machines and teletypesetting machines like the ones described above. Headline or display material requiring a larger point size and fewer characters was generally still set by hand composition. Whether hand-composed with foundry type or mechanically composed with brass matrices and cast slugs, text matter was generated and reproduced from three-dimensional metal letterforms (as opposed to the two-dimensional film matrix letterforms that would come later).

By the end of the nineteenth century there were fifteen hundred registered patents for typesetting gadgetry. Many unsuccessful attempts were made to develop effective typesetting machinery. The Paige typesetting machine, "which Mark Twain said could do the work of six men except drink, swear, and go out on strike,"[3] cost a fortune to manufacture, had nearly twenty thousand moving parts, and sent its owners into bankruptcy.

The most successful of the hot-metal linecasting machines was the Linotype, invented and patented by Ottmar Mergenthaler in 1885. Mergenthaler's machine was commercially successful and its use widespread (seventy-four thousand typesetters were sold from 1893 through 1968),[4] so much so that "Linotype" is now used in a generic sense, much like Johnson and Johnson's "Band-aids" and Kimberly-Clark's "Kleenex."

Considering that Mergenthaler's patent for automated typesetting was preceded by fifty-seven patents for machines of similar design,[5] the assembling of a line of type, or matrices, with a mechanism actuated by keyboard tapping was not novel in 1885. What was novel, according to the United States Patent Office, was the combination of a matrix and casting mechanism in one machine. The United States circuit court of appeals was satisfied in ruling that, "Mergenthaler was the first to combine a mechanism for forming a matrix composed of a series of dies adapted for transposition or rearrangement, [with] a mold and a casting mechanism." In the court's view, Mergenthaler was the "first to produce a practical machine by which ordinary hand composition was superseded."[6] Seen from an employer's perspective, the advantages of the Linotype were sizeable: the machine increased the output of hand composition threefold. The time-consuming task of distribution (putting used type back in the case) was obviated since cast type was recycled via the "hellbox" and melted down. Slugs of cast type were created anew, thereby supplying clean, crisp letterforms for printing.

By 1987, Monotype and Linotype machines were virtually extinct—dinosaurs of the trade. That such machines are technologically obsolete is evident in the act of their having been elevated to the status of museum object. When the *Washington Post* built its new office building, the architect placed a polished and painted Linotype machine in the street-entrance lobby. The machine now serves as an ornamental sculpture that authenticates the past.[7] Joe Malady describes a similar situation at the newspaper where he worked: "In Atlantic City, they nickel-plated the last Linotype machine. They kept it in the front office . . . kind of like a memento of the times."[8]

Heritage Printers: A Dinosaur Lives

One place where these typecasting machines can still be found in working condition is at Heritage Printers in Charlotte, North Carolina. Established in 1956 by William E. Loftin, Heritage is one of the few printing establishments to remain an exclusively hot-metal plant.

It is November 1986 when I visit Heritage. Since the printers employed here are still working in the same technology of their apprenticeships, I go expecting to find less nostalgia in their talk of the trade.

There is no sign designating the business. Bill Loftin would later explain the lack of signage as intentional—a way of discouraging local requests for job printing (which they do not do)—and add jokingly, "in the early days, to help keep away my creditors."

I find the establishment with little trouble, having gotten telephone directions from the receptionist. The front door is kept locked and a hand-lettered sign reads: "Please Knock." Cathy Parris comes to the door and I am welcomed with unanticipated enthusiasm. "You must be Maggie. They've been expecting you. They've been so excited about your coming and have all sorts of things prepared for you."

Cathy takes my coat and umbrella. I can hear men talking in a nearby office and in a minute Bill Loftin comes out. Bill is a

Fig. 32. Heritage Printers of Charlotte, North Carolina, 1986. Photo by the author.

handsome Southern gentleman, with silky white hair and generous blue eyes. He introduces himself and then a man his senior, Earl Powell, before inviting us into his office. "This is the man you want to talk to."

In his early eighties, Earl now oversees operations as "Ambassador" at Washburn Graphics, a local advertising and printing plant where he has spent fifty-one of his fifty-four years in the printing trade. Earl tells some stories of his early days. His love of the business is infectious.

After taking care of some business Bill walks in and grabs a seat, saying, "I want to hear about all of this!"

". . . the Monotype Casters was the noisiest part of the composing room back then. And Mr. Loftin's got some Monotypes back there. Still the finest typesetting system that was ever devised." I notice that Earl's way of speaking stresses continuity. He does not drop his tone at predictable intervals. His accent and voice, slow and drawn out, differ from those of the rest of the employees. He stresses the first syllable of words like "ideas" and "afternoon," revealing his deep Southern heritage.

"You could do things with the Monotype that you can't do with Linotype."

"Spacing-wise?" I ask.

"Well, spacing-wise, tabular matter and that sort of thing. With Monotype you could hold the true character of the design." Bill joins in, "One of the features of Monotype is that it *prints* so much better than Linotype, because you're only casting that one character. Whereas in Linotype, you're casting sixty or seventy or eighty characters at one shot. So that Linotype slug, as it's called, might be higher on one end than on the other and fatter on one end than the other. And when you get to the press, it doesn't print evenly."

"Well, it can be *made* to print evenly. That's where the pressman has to show his stuff, in the make-ready."[9] Sounds of leads being sawed drift in from the large open room adjacent to Bill's office. "But even at that, it is never *as* sharp or *as* good as printing from Monotype. We're going to run the Monotype for you this morning. We don't run it every day, we just run it on demand."

Earl's deeper voice adds, "Oh, you're going to enjoy that."

"I've never seen Monotype," I confess.

"Most fascinating machine ever built," Earl says with great satisfaction.

Bill attests, "It's unbelievable."

"Is it hard to get parts for it?"

"Well, we cannibalize. You can buy some parts, but the machine is no longer made in this country."

The three of us walk out of Bill's office through a small corridor into what serves as a combination mailroom, storage room, and employee lunchroom. There are two vending machines and a microwave oven. Down at the far end of the room are two Ludlow type cases, a Ludlow caster, and the Monotype keyboard. I am introduced to Rick Newell, a relatively young foreman, who joins us from the other room. We stand around the Monotype keyboard.

Fig. 33. Monotype keyboard. Photo by the author.

Bill explains, "In Monotype, you've got a two-stage operation. You've got the keyboard and the caster. On the Linotype, it's
all part of one machine." I have read this many times but to see
these components, physically separated in two different rooms,
clarifies the operation.

"Also, I want you to notice that there are two keyboards. One
is for the roman and one is for the italic.

"And the reason it has its own keyboard is that everything in
Monotype is done on a unit system. It's like the first computer."

Rick nods. "Really, yeah."

"This goes back a hundred years. But it really is sort of a
computer."

Like a circus barker, Earl throws in, "That was the world's
first computer!"

Bill raises his eyebrows. "It really is." He stands back and
explains the keyboard's relationship to the individual typefaces and
the mechanics of word spacing. "When you get to the end of a

line, you take a reading off of this dial up here. Then you punch in a code. And what that code does is set the caster so it will cut a word space that will give a justified line. And I still don't believe it, but it does.

"Now in Linotype," Bill continues, "to justify a line is simple. I'll show you why. In this," he points to the Monotype keyboard, "every different character is a different piece of metal. So you've got to come out with twenty-six picas! Somehow. Which means that those word spaces have got to be accurate. In the Linotype, it'll be twenty-six picas but it's very simple to get it." Rick adds, "It's done all at once by pushing the spaceband bar. *This,* each one is separate."

"If you don't know," says Bill, "word spacing in lines varies. Take a line on a page—the word spacing varies slightly. That's where you get rivers in pages because you get *too* much word spacing. And that's where you separate the men from the boys in typesetting. Operators that can give you no rivers. That involves sometimes going back and setting three lines back and two lines forwards."

We follow Bill into the back room. It has the feel of a mechanic's garage: grease, dirt, and oil, partially disassembled parts, cast-iron machinery. There are five Monotype machines and hundreds of Monotype matrix cases stacked nearby. I smell molten lead. Bill explains that though Monotype lead should be harder, they use Linotype pigs in the Monotype caster crucible. I notice a mat case on the table and tell him I have seen pictures of these but never could visualize how they were used.

Earl enters the room proclaiming, "Now this is the fascination machine," as Bill continues to explain the Monotype system. "This is the mat case which holds the matrices. One thing about this, you only need one matrix for each character, 'cause you're only casting one. In Linotype, you gotta have twenty lowercase *e*'s. 'Cause in one line, you might have five *e*'s."

Reminiscent of a train conductor who knows the timetable like the back of his hand, Powell recites the following statistics. "That's 255 characters in the 15–15 and 275 in the 17–17." Bill

Fig. 34. Monotype machine. Photo by the author.

explains, "Now what you mean by 15–15 is 15 character rows this way and 15 rows that way."

We turn around. Behind us are two Monotype machines side by side. We gather around the one against the wall. Bill points to the roll of paper ribbon resembling a piano roll. "Now what the tape does is position the mat case in here over the mold, which is stationary. And the holes [in the paper roll] tell the machine which row down and which row across."

Earl jokes, "The movingest machine that was ever invented."

"The what, Earl?" asks Bill.

"The moving-est."

Bill smiles and turns to me. "It makes a wonderful sound. You ought to record it. I've been wanting to record the sound of this thing." Speaking of sounds, I inquire about the constant hissing I hear.

"What's that air sound?"

"Compressed air. The metal comes up from underneath the case. It's in liquid state there, 550 degrees." Earl adds, "It's a little hotter than Linotype." I look down into the well of metallic-grey molten alloy. Earl bends down explaining, "See, the pistons go up and down and pump," while Bill tells us, "I don't know as much about this as these fellows do and I'm doing all the talking."

"Sure you do," says Rick, and Bill, reassured, continues. "The whole works is moving to position that mat case, to cast. To level it off, it has a blade that shaves the bottom of it off so that everything is perfectly 918." [10]

"All right." Bill gives the go-ahead.

Rick has the Monotype all set to go. "Ready to roll," he says as he flips a switch. "Be sure if everything's right. This thing even scares me."

Earl, proud of the machine, announces, "It casts a line up to ten inches, too." Suddenly, the machine comes alive—a wonderful mechanical sound of chinking and revolving parts, like someone shaking a cigar box full of marbles. We stand around marveling at the machine's synchronized movement and Bill says, "The guy that put that together had to be a genius."

"Oh yeah," says Rick, but Earl's got dates and names. "Tolbert Lanston, 1887."

The galley is filling up with metal characters. I ask Rick about the water I see dripping.

"That cools the mold. That keeps it nice and cool. If it gets too hot, it squirts."

Bill says, "We've got four systems here: We've got gas that heats the metal, air that reads the compression, electricity to run the motor, and water to cool it." I notice the individual characters inching their way forward and ask, "Now those characters, are they fusing together?"

"Each one is separate," Rick tells me. Earl adds, "Just like hand-set type." Rick holds up one letter and indeed, it looks a good bit like foundry type.

Bill pulls down a rectangular box from a nearby shelf. He opens it up to show us. "These are matrices for caps in larger sizes on this caster over here." He turns around and introduces me to another machine. "It's sort of like the Ludlow. It's just a caster, one letter at a time."

He opens up the box in his hand. "That is 24 point Goudy Oldstyle italic. But what makes this a prize is, we bought these for a dollar a box. They were closing up a shop in Philadelphia. Just think of it—all of civilization, you might say, is provided in that one box there." I look up and realize that there is an entire shelf full of these matrix boxes.

"That's progress," he adds with gentle sarcasm.

Listening and watching the Monotype, one can see the derivation of a hot-metal term like "leading," which has survived the transition to cold composition even though the lead strips have no place in computerized phototypesetting. Bill and Earl continue to describe the inner workings of this wonder machine. The more I hear, the more I realize that comprehension is probably in the doing of it.

We have spent enough time here. Bill motions for us to continue along. We walk back through the common mail-lunch-storage room and make our way into the largest space in the plant.

Fig. 35. Printers' case rack for storage of foundry type. Photo by the author.

It is a rectangular room, roughly thirty by one hundred feet. This is also the most active area of the plant. Men are keyboarding on Linotype machines, others are making up galleys and pulling proofs. In the back end of the room are many wooden and metal cabinets where font after font of foundry type is stored.

I notice that the windows around the room are papered over and that the light is fluorescent. The eight Linotype machines have additional light fixtures with high-intensity bulbs. Three Linotypes are running. Bill takes me over to one where a man is busy at work.

The sound this machine makes is somewhat softer, lighter, and higher in pitch than the Monotype. Bill introduces me to the operator. "This is Maggie Holtzberg and this is Lindy Floyd. Charles 'Lindberg' Floyd," Bill adds, and chuckles. I would later learn that Lindy, as well as another employee at Heritage, Joe Earnhardt, were both raised at the same orphanage, where they were trained as printers. Nicknaming orphans after famous people was common there.

I pronounce my last name slowly, over the din of Linotype noise. Bill goes back to explaining how the machine differs from the one we just observed.

"Anyway, in Linotype, here's the metal, right here . . ." We step around to the left side of the machine. ". . . down in there, in the crucible." An oblong "pig" is suspended from above on a chain and is half melted into the crucible. Lindy informs me that he may go through half a dozen pigs in one day.

The smell of the lead alloy is thick. Bill narrates the process. "The metal is drawn off. Now when it casts, the crucible comes up against the mold here. See, the plunger goes down? Pumps the metal. Cools enough to form solid. Ejects it." As he says this, a line of type drops from the chute. I go to feel the temperature. "That's hot," Bill warns. I move instead toward the lines in the far left of the slug tray. "The closer you get over there, the hotter it is.

"The keyboard releases the matrix out of the magazine. It comes down into the lineholder right here." We watch as individ-

Fig. 36. Lindy Floyd at the Linotype. Photo by the author.

ual matrices join the forming line. "When he gets his line full, it transfers over into the casting division. The spacebands, coming over, now see those spacebands coming over? That's what justifies the line."

"It's just random?" I ask. "Between words?"

"It would be the same amount between each word. Let's have a spaceband, Lindy." To my surprise, Lindy lifts one out from the line he is assembling and hands it to Bill. "See, it has a flap in the bottom? It comes over to the casting position. An arm comes up and fits into those spacebands. And it's tapered, you see?"

At intervals the space bands rise up. "See 'em come up?"

"Yep."

"As it jams everything at both ends. And that's how it justifies." I recall Carl Gross telling me how there is nothing like seeing those spacebands push up, squeezing the line out, to learn the meaning of justify. Lindy picks up a slug and shows it to me. "Now see this? There's your name." He hands me six pi mats held together with scotch tape.

"You spelled it right!"

"How 'bout that?" Some mats fall, or "pi," to use the colloquial, and I ask Bill how they get redistributed.

"Well, I'll show you. That's the real invention that Mergenthaler made, the circulating matrix. So that you can get continuous typesetting while you're setting one line, the line ahead of it is being cast, and the line ahead of *that* is being distributed for reuse. So it's a circulating matrix. That kernel of an idea, that's what made all the difference in the world. They could cast from a matrix but it didn't distribute them back."

There is a flurry of movement. Brass and metal parts, clattering, tottering, jingling into position—a complex and rich ensemble of loosely moving parts.

"All right, it's coming over. It's justified. That was a tight line." I ask about the lay of the keyboard, which has three color-coded sections. Lindy responds, "The blue keys are numbers, punctuation. The caps are white. Also, you see, we have two po-

Fig. 37. Linotype keyboard. Photo by the author.

sitions. There's roman, and up is italic. Or bold. Could be small caps."

I watch him tap the keys and remark at how fast he is. After I ask about the space bar, Bill instructs me to watch the space-bands coming down. "Plunger goes down into the mold. The mold is in the mold disc and the matrix hits against the face of the mold. That leaves the character standing up on the slug. And that's where you get the idea of letterpress. It's still quite an invention," he adds. "We ought to set her name."

"Okay," says Lindy. "I remember the last, what was the first?"

"M-a-g-g-i-e."

"Maggie, Maggie," he says to himself as his fingers tap.

"And what face are you in?" I ask.

"Caledonia."

While we are waiting for the line to be cast, Bill notices one he is dissatisfied with in the galley. "Boy, that's a loose one. You try not to have that. That's an unusual situation there. You can see it too." He addresses Lindy, "What was going on in that line, Lindy?" I am suddenly aware that Bill is Lindy's boss.

"That was one that they couldn't get another word on." He turns to me, dissipating the criticism with an explanation. "In other words, when you get to the end of a line, if you can't divide the word you've got to space it out. That's what the spacebands do, really. If they're not big enough, then you have to add extra space."

A new slug drops out. "That's hot, feel it," Bill says. I do, as he reassures me, "It's not so hot." I ask Lindy, "Do you ever burn yourself?"

"No more," he says and smiles.

"As a beginner?" I add.

"Right. This is 550 degrees."

Bill reads the slug out loud, "Maggie Holtzberg, Heritage Printers, November 13, 1986." Lindy suggests someone getting me a proof of it but Bill responds, "She might not want ink on it." We laugh about that and Lindy offers to reset it. "Besides," he says, "you can wash the ink off. And you can read it better if you have a little ink on it anyway. Take the glare out.

"I'm half blind," he adds.

I sympathize, "You must be, it must be tiring on your eyes."

"It is. Well I mean after all these years. I've been doing it all my life."

But Bill reminds us of the alternatives. "I don't think it's as tiring as those terminals in phototypesetting. It has that green cast. Gosh."

I agree. Lindy tells me that he had worked in photocomposition for a few years. The place where he was working switched over from hot metal. "It was like trying to teach an old dog new tricks," he tells me. "I didn't like it."

What makes this printer's reaction to new technology particularly interesting is that, unlike the majority of printers his age, he has been free to remain in the hot-metal environment. He has not been displaced, nor experienced occupational discontinuity.

His preference for the former technology—the nineteenth-century mechanized typecasting machine—is realized in his daily work.

And what of the nineteenth-century printer? What satisfaction did he derive from hand composition and how did the introduction of this automated typecasting machine affect him? It is difficult to know what work was like in a different time and a different technology. We have historical accounts and labor statistics, we have memoirs and fictional sketches, we have the testimony of revivalist hobby printers, enthusiasts by nature, and we have the material record—the printed page.

Handpeggers versus Linotype Operators

One gets a sense of the pace and challenge of the hand compositor's work by reading a nineteenth-century diary, kept by an "old printer" employed in the composing room at *Harper's*. Daily, he sets, corrects, and distributes type, recording "fat" and "lean" jobs along with his rate of pay for weekly versus piecework. For this man pride and satisfaction are gained through handsetting "clean" copy at a quick pace:

"April 25, [1871].—I set up a page by 11 o'clock, distributed till almost 3, corrected a proof, and set a little over half a page more. I can't get up two pages, the best I can do; but I set more than the fellow next to me. He had a bad false motion, and I have kept watch of the time it would take each of us to set a line, and also a stickful, and I always gain on him, although he makes much faster motions than I do."

There is also much joy derived in setting significant prose. "The principal event of the day was my getting some copy written by William Cullen Bryant, the poet. . . . I can now say that I have set the great poet's manuscript."[11]

In two decades' time, the era of the hand compositor would be drawing to a close. Many printers worried that the machine would curtail the amount of labor required in the composing room. Newspapers across the country were investing in mechanized typecasting, leaving many employees feeling threatened and angry.

John Hicks's *Adventures of a Tramp Printer* provides a personalized view of what the old-time practical printers experienced. Though a fictionalized account, Hicks's narrative is based on the author's experience as a field representative for the International Typographical Union and his acquaintance with the union's older members who had lived through the transition from hand- to machine-set type. The protagonist's life story is a composite, "his name is legion." His travels and experiences are presented as typical of a tramp printer's adventures in the hand-set days. The year is 1889, the town, Boston:

> Machines were in use on several of the country's newspapers, demonstrating that type could be set mechanically, even though it wasn't being done as we had visualized it. No fearful and wonderful mechanism with myriad antennae was seated on the tall stool of the printer, picking up the types and assembling them in the composing sticks. As a matter of fact, there was no type, as we knew type, connected with it. Matrices ran down channels and were assembled to cast a whole line of type at one time. They called it the Linotype. For the old hand peggers, whose forte had been the setting of "straight matter" on daily newspapers, it spelled finis. [12]

Prideful, resentful, this old-time printer expresses his opposition to the invention responsible for supplanting people and their handicraft skills: "It might have been the rum and gum talking, but I asserted I would quit typesetting before the machines took my job away from me. . . . We had been lulled by the fatuous belief that no machine could ever do our work, but discovered we had been living in fool's paradise." [13]

He is resolved to give up the trade if need be, rather than compromise his identity as a typesetter:

> [Ollie] Hicks said I might learn to run one of the new machines, but I told him I was a typesetter, not a piano player, and

further that they were not going to put a pot of hot lead on my shoulder and let the type run down my sleeve. I would throw my stick and my rule in the channel, I told them, and forthwith started out. They followed, making a little procession of it, and we saluted Ben Franklin as we passed his statue in Milk Street. Arriving at the channel, I threw the implements of my trade as far out into the water as I could, at the same time saying, "I hereby solemnly renounce typesetting as a means of gaining a livelihood, and pledge my honor never to again touch type." [14]

A slightly less bitter, yet sympathetic view is expressed in verse by hand compositor Edward D. Berry. His use of "back in eighty-fo'" signifies the pre-machine era. The strange spellings and contractions may have been Berry's attempt to capture a Southern dialect. The word "dis." in stanza 1 is an abbreviation for "distribute." Five out of the original seven stanzas appear below.

Musings of an Old Time Printer

Ah recolleck, 'way back in eight-fo',
Th' things we used t' do t' make a string.
'Twas "dis." all day
An' plug away
All night, t' make ouah dollah-ninety-fo'.

Them days is gone—no mo' th' call
   o' "Time"
Ah'll heah, like music t' my eah.
Yep, Thirty's on the hook,
Them days is like a book
That's out o' print—anothah day is heah.

Ah stan; an' look in wondah while them boys,
With dancing fingahs, pound a lot o' keys,
A-settin' up a string
O' type that ought t' bring
T' them a life of plutocratic ease.

But shucks! They ain't a-settin' type at all!
They're punchin' holes in paper; they ring a bell,

Let loose a lot o' air,
An' sit there in a chair
With a cushion on it, an' think they're raisin' hell!

Th' good ol' days have sho'ly passed away,
An' printin' as Ah knew it ain't no mo';
But Ah live in recollection
An' mou'n the sad deflection
Of how we used t' print, in eighty-fo'. [15]

Enthusiasm for the "hand-pegged" days may seem little more than nostalgia, but for printers to identify themselves or others with the era of hand composition is like invoking the golden age of printing. I am reminded of the morning that I met with Joe Malady in the lobby of the Union Printers Home. We had been chatting about the transition to computer typesetting when a small-framed Hispanic man walked up. He was toting his oxygen tank with him, his "ball and chain," he called it. Indeed, it is his life line.

"Philipo, what's happening?" Joe introduces me to Philadelphia Valdez. "This young lady is trying to get some idea of what the printers think of the cold type."

Fil, as his friends call him, answers, "Well, most of us went through the transition period. We started out from the old hand-pegged days and continued through to the computer era."

Joe admits to Fil, "I never went through the handset stage, but I did go through the Linotype."

Fil looks incredulously at Joe and asks him point blank, "You didn't go through the hand pegged? You never lived!" [16]

Union printers were reluctant to accept mechanization. In 1899, when the *New York Sun* hired nonunion printers to operate the newly installed Linotype machines, No. 6 went out on strike for thirty-one months. [17] The union negotiated the use of mechanized typecasters with the stipulation that journeymen printers man the machines. Because of the union's labor-market monopoly of craft skills and the economic position of the printing industry, the ITU was able to insist its members receive an equitable share of benefits brought by the new technology: shorter hours, higher wages, and improved conditions. [18]

Nearly a century later, compositors would be facing a new threatening machine—the electronic word processor. One might well hear the assertion: "I am a Linotype operator, not a typist!" Hot-metal compositors had grown accustomed to the Linotype's keyboard and its pot of hot lead. Speed and accuracy persist as motivating concerns. Clean copy and a quick pace can challenge the Linotype operator.

Cynthia Cockburn relays the words of English Linotype operators in her book on the impact of technological change in the London newspaper world: "It has never felt boring to me. You are always trying to set cleaner than you did the day before." . . . "What did I enjoy? Just the pure effortless flow of stringing words and sentences together. How can I put it? I suppose it was a revelry, it was the ease and speed with which I personally felt I could get galleys of stuff out and when it came back from the reader there would be just one, maybe two mistakes in it, that's all." [19]

Though the work process was semiautomated, the Linotype operator enjoyed an interactive relationship with his machine; like the mechanically inclined owner of an automobile, he felt that it was his to tinker with and clean.

A passage from John Updike's novel *Rabbit Redux* captures the symbiotic quality of the compositor's work on the Linotype machine:

> The machine stands tall and warm above him, mothering, muttering, a temperamental thousand-parted survival from the golden age of machinery. The sorts tray is on his right hand; the Star Quadder and the mold disc and slug tray on his left; a green-shaded light bulb at the level of his eyes. . . . all these rustling sighing tons of intricately keyed mass waiting for the feather-touch of his intelligence. Behind the mold disc the molten lead waits; sometimes when there is a jam the lead squirts hot out: Harry has been burned. But the machine is a baby; its demands, though inflexible, are few, and once these demands are met obedi-

Fig. 38. Lindy Floyd making adjustments on his Linotype. Photo by the author.

ence automatically follows. There is no problem with fidelity. Do for it, it does for you.[20]

There are those, however, who recount their work at the Linotype as boring. When the machines were first introduced, some say they fared badly in comparison to hand composition. Labor historian George Barnett wrote that "[t]he one unfavorable effect of the machine from the standpoint of the workman is the increase in the intensity of labor. Linotype operators are universally agreed that machine work is far more exhausting than hand composition."[21]

In addition, some printers feel that the Linotype significantly limits the craftsman's capability to affect aesthetic decisions. A journeyman stonecutter, accustomed to the tactile immediacy of creating letterforms with chisel, mallet, and stone, explains:

"The problem with machines is they distance man from his aesthetic sensibility. Take the Linotype. Tools are infinitely removed from the hand and the eye. The more you distance the tool from the hand and eye, the less opportunity you have to exercise refined aesthetic judgment.

"The Linotype was the first of the composing machines to limit aesthetic judgment. You sat down and keyboarded and when it came time to justify the line, the spacing was just zapped in. It was a modular form of spacing. They didn't go on and say, 'How can we improve on this, how can we alter the spacing in an aesthetic way?' whereas on Monotype, you can go back to one line and alter uniquely the pieces of spacing. There was a moment at which the Monotype operator put the job on the slab [stone] and altered it. With the Linotype, you made your spacing decisions on the machine, rather than on the slab."[22]

Partial automation of the composition process may decrease one's freedom to make adjustments, but the hot-type compositor is still left with typographical decisions to make and a degree of manual labor to do. Questions of justification and word breaks remain under the Linotype or Monotype operator's control, unlike his current-day counterpart for whom end-of-line decisions involving justification and hyphenation are relinquished to a computer programmer.

The Linotype and Monotype operators' productivity is tangible. As Hugh Williamson has so nicely put it, "typesetting in metal can be seen and heard and, indeed, smelt, and is more easily understood through the senses than are the silent and hygienic mysteries of electronics."[23] For the generation of printers apprenticed in hot-metal composing rooms, working with metal brings unique satisfaction. Part of this may be due to the influence of initial experience and the power of nostalgia. When book designer and printer Greer Allen asked himself why he had a particular devotion to the former hot-metal technology, he attributed it, in part, to the timing of his career:

"The reason that I have such a devotion to the old ways and other people don't is because I am recalled to the time when I first entered the field. You know, I've worked all my life to get back to be able to do, in a sense, the things that drew me into the field in the first place. It was to do these things with my hands. What attracted me to printing was not imagery and forms and space and all that gobbledegook about design, but it was simply the doing of it. And the doing of it and getting this lovely thing. And getting it over and over again.

"It's a matter of when you were born into that technology and then you want to go back to it in a certain point in life. And it does inform everything you do through the changing years. And so you work to get back to those roots all the time." [24]

Formative training certainly colors one's attitude toward technology, but hot metal holds an additional appeal attributable to more than nostalgia. It has to do with what supplanted hot metal, namely photocomposition and offset printing. From a reader's point of view, these processes often produce weak, spineless letterforms. Listen to people discussing letterpress printing and you will hear enraptured talk about "that third dimension." Run your hand over a letterpress printed page and you can *feel* the impression of metal on dampened paper.

The anthropomorphic vitality of letterpress printing has taken on larger-than-life significance for the cognoscenti. The passive, push-button world of cold composition is a weak substitute in the eyes of small-press publisher Harry Duncan, who expresses his views in an interview with editor Robert Dana:

"Most of the ways in which literature comes to us nowadays look to me anemic. If you bother to look at it, it almost disappears off the page."

When asked what he means by "anemic," Duncan responds, "It just doesn't have any guts to it. . . . I'm talking about a certain reassuring presence in the quality of ink and the third-dimensional quality of type penetrating paper, because those are things that really did exist as objects. With photo-offset printing, everything is spiritual . . . nothing is embodied, quite. A book is a physical thing. It is the contents of the book which has its soul."

Dana, trying to take his meaning, says, ". . . the printing of the type is too pale."

"Yes. It doesn't have very much presence in space . . . the

only means that we know of for a natural evolution of alphabetic forms is through handcraft. The alphabet is not an intellectual matter. It is a matter physically realized by the hands of men. Like shoes or fabrics. And maybe someday we'll assign computers the right task, the right problems to solve, and get back some graphic presence in books."[25]

This sentiment of the need to retrieve a lost graphic presence finds expression in the following bit of office folklore. This "obituary" was posted on the University of Illinois Press bulletin board, most likely by a member of the production department:

OBITUARY

In Memoriam

Typography, Art of—Died recently and suddenly after being devoured by predators in the PC environment.

Typography, who never had any nickname on record, attained a certain celebrity status in the '70s and '80s, following the introduction of "The Godchild," otherwise known across the land as "cold-type." Typography's health was known to have grown more delicate in recent years, although Typography's untimely death still came as a surprise, according to a family spokesperson.

Another family member, however, reports that an apparent hereditary illness, said to eventually cripple its victims, has afflicted several close relatives. This includes twin first cousins, Syntax and Spelling. A sibling, Word Breaks, is reported institutionally insane. All are said to have been at one time closely involved in the family business.

Typography is survived, among others, by all the many brothers and sisters of the now-deceased Local 21.

Cash contribution memorials may be donated to any needy alumnus.[26]

From a printer's point of view, the rewards of working in metal parallel the reader's satisfaction. A harmony of voices sings its praises:

Bob Culp, former Linotype operator and stoneman, recalled,

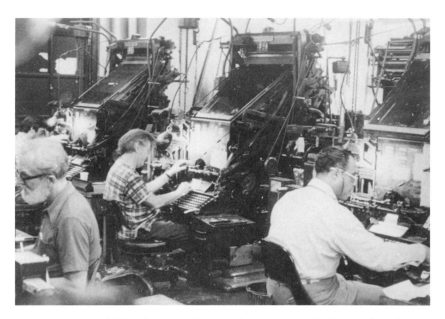

Fig. 39. *New York Times* hot-metal composing room, 1978. Photo taken during the filming of the documentary *Farewell Etaoin Shrdlu*. Used with permission of Carl Schlesinger.

"When we completed a job, that was hours of work—setting type, lock-up with wood and metal. It was a work of art. You *signed* your work.

"It was the inventiveness of the thing. Working with *raw materials,* so that even when we changed over to paper, the knowledge, the depth of knowledge was carried over."[27]

English compositors noted, "You could feel you were involved with a base material, creating something out of it, like a carpenter with wood."

"There's a weight behind it. You lock up the frame, pick it up—it may weigh a couple of hundredweight. And you feel as if you have achieved something."

"There is the actual physical effort of cutting up rules, figuring out the best way to do a thing, going and choosing type. It's artistic. A good comp is an artist as well as working with his hands, like Michelangelo, I suppose."[28]

Earl Powell, printer, reminisced, "Well, I just enjoyed the *feel* of the type and the chance to try and make something look good, something that would please the client.

"It was just a great feeling to me to handle those slugs and be able to put 'em together and space them properly and choose the right headings and the right display to make it work out right and be pleasing to the eye." [29]

Dan Burns, retired stonehand, said proudly, "I used to enjoy setting an ad and having accomplished something. Making it look pretty. Making it look right. Using the right style of type, coming out nice, then having somebody say, 'Boy, that's nice.' Which I have had done to me." [30]

When Dan Burns retired in 1961 he was fifty-six years of age, which made him eighty-one when I went to see him. Though a good bit younger, Bob Culp had worked with Dan Burns and he respected his craftsmanship. They were of different generations. This meant that when photocomposition arrived, Dan was among those printers who did not retrain. For a printer who did retrain, Bob knew the cost of being left behind in a dying craft: "Some guys didn't make it. It hurt, physically and emotionally; it did them in. It would be like going to a great artist and taking away his brushes."

Bob Culp is not alone in his assessment of the change to cold type. Carl Schlesinger, a longtime veteran of the composing room at the *New York Times,* and the man responsible for retraining many of the printers there, described the conversion: "It radically changed the working lives of millions. Their tools were taken away from them."

Schlesinger made this comment during a viewing of the film *Farewell Etaoin Shrdlu,* at the New York Public Library. The film documents the *New York Times* overnight switch to computer typesetting in 1978. [31] Editors, printers, stereotypers, and pressmen are interviewed on camera during production of the last edition of the *Times* ever to be set in hot-metal type. The immediacy of the historical moment gives great weight to the journeymen's words, as they voice their feelings about adapting their skills to the

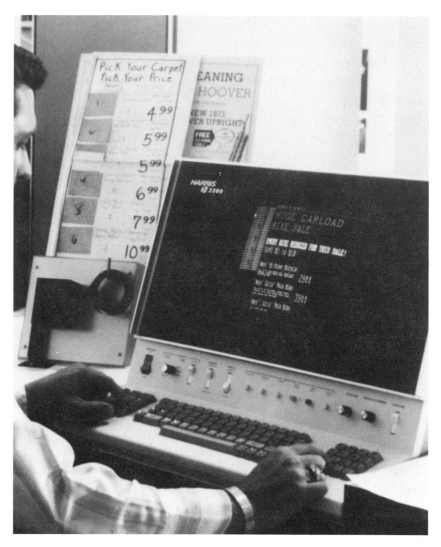

Fig. 40. The new technology at the *New York Times*, 1978. Photo taken during the filming of the documentary *Farewell Etaoin Shrdlu*. Used with permission of Carl Schlesinger.

change. The film captures the grit and dirt, the smear of ink, and the eyes, hands, and minds of humans interacting with hot-metal machines. The old methods are then contrasted with the new. Printers are seen retrained, composing images by electronics, and running computer-driven videotypesetters.

The seemingly esoteric title of the film derives from hot-metal practice. The phrase "etaoin shrdlu" was produced by lightly tapping the first twelve keys on the Linotype machine keyboard. Running one's fingers down these keys was a quick way of completing a line which had an error in it. The line could then be discarded.

For a hot-metal printer, "etaoin shrdlu" is anything but esoteric. Amelia Story surprised herself by being able to recite the string of vowels and consonants after so many years. "I learned those letters: e-t-a-o-i-n-s-h-r-d-l-u-c-m-f-w-y-p. I can still run 'em off, you know." [32]

To say farewell "etaoin shrdlu" is to say hello to cold type.

Notes

1. There was such a thing known as a cold-metal typemaking machine. It was developed around the time of the early linecasters and required a very soft metal (e.g., pure lead) which would be forced into a die to form individual letters. The method proved impractical. See *Carroll T. Harris: Conversations on Type and Printing, 1967,* interview conducted by Ruth Teiser (University of California, Berkeley, Bancroft Library, Regional Oral History Office, 1976), 33.

2. For a concise, historical review of union/management confrontations over the introduction of TTS and electronic typesetting devices, see Andrew Zimbalist, ed., *Case Studies on the Labor Process* (New York: Monthly Review Press, 1979), 103–26.

3. Anthony Smith, *Goodbye Gutenberg: The Newspaper Revolution of the 1980s* (New York: Oxford University Press, 1980), 211.

4. Seybold, *World of Digital Typesetting,* 40.

5. Richard Huss, "Typesetting Machines and Ancillary Equipment, 1822–1925," quoted in Seybold, *World of Digital Typesetting,* 40.

6. "Linotype Patents Sustained on Final Appeal, December 1894," United

States Circuit Court of Appeals, Third Circuit, *The Rogers Typography Company, Appellant, v. The Mergenthaler Linotype Company.*

7. I wish to thank Archie Green for bringing this to my attention.

8. Joe Malady, tape-recorded interview, 2 February 1988.

9. The "make-ready" is the printer's term for securing a firm, even impression of a form in the press. To achieve this the pressman uses tiny pieces of paper to build up lower parts and cuts down higher ones that are printing too heavy.

10. All type is of uniform height. Bill's use of "918" refers to .918, or approximately ¹¹⁄₁₂ of an inch in height. This is the measurement from the feet or base of the type to the face, or printing surface, and is the standard printing height-to-paper of lead type in America.

11. "Diary of an Old Printer: The Intimate Experiences of a Composing-room Worker at Harper's in New York Half a Century Ago," *The American Printer* 70, no. 5 (5 March 1920).

12. John Edward Hicks, *Adventures of a Tramp Printer, 1880–1890* (Kansas City, Mo.: Midamerican Press, 1950), 275–76.

13. Ibid., 280.

14. Ibid., 281.

15. Edward D. Berry, poem published in souvenir book, 1934, on occasion of 78th ITU Annual Convention.

16. Tape-recorded exchange in the lobby of the Union Printers Home, 2 February 1988.

17. Zimbalist, *Case Studies,* 121.

18. See Kelber and Schlesinger, *Union Printers and Controlled Automation,* chapter 1, and George Barnett, "The Printers: A Study in American Trade Unionism," *American Economic Quarterly,* 3rd Series X, no. 3 (1909): 198.

19. Cockburn, *Brothers,* 48–49.

20. John Updike, *Rabbit Redux* (New York: Ballantine Books, 1971, 4th printing, 1985), 35. The protagonist in this novel, Harry Angstrom, is employed at a newspaper plant which is undergoing the transition from hot to cold composition.

21. Barnett, "The Printers," 202.

22. Richard Grasby, journeyman lettercutter, personal communication, 13 February 1986. Carl Schlesinger takes issue with Grasby's complaint, saying that "in later years (1920s onwards) many modifications, such as ¼ point spacing between letters, one-character mats (true-cut for a font), and special ligatures for kerned characters were produced which gave the Linotype product the aesthetics of fine printing." Personal communication, February 1990.

23. Hugh Williamson, *Methods of Book Design* (New Haven: Yale University Press, 1983), 67.

24. Greer Allen, Adjunct Professor in Graphic Arts, Yale School of Art

[formerly the Yale University Printer]. Interview at his home, 22 February 1986.

25. Quoted from *Against the Grain: Interviews with Maverick American Publishers* (Iowa City: University of Iowa Press, 1986), 60–61.

26. Sent to me by executive editor Judith McCulloh. Source unknown.

27. Bob Culp, told to me during work, 12 August 1985.

28. Examples taken from Cockburn, *Brothers*, 51.

29. Earl Powell, tape-recorded interview at Heritage Printers, 13 November 1986.

30. Dan Burns, tape-recorded interview at his home, 13 September 1985.

31. Carl Schlesinger served as technical advisor and narrator of the film. The film (29 minutes, color, 1980) was written, directed, produced, and edited by David Loeb Weiss. It is available through the Museum of Modern Art, New York City.

32. Amelia Story, tape-recorded interview, 3 February 1988.

5

The Change: Cold Composition

Up until the advent of photocomposition (1950s) and microprocessors (1970s), type composition had remained essentially the same for the five centuries following the invention of movable type (1440s). The industrial revolution of the nineteenth century did not in fact lead to any revolution in printing. As recently as 1967, the industrial sociologist A. J. M. Sykes could write, "gradual change there has been but even today the industry is far from completely mechanized; for example, most compositors still work by hand and serve their apprenticeships as hand compositors. As mechanization has not led to any major change in skills, the basic trades of compositor and printer remain fundamentally unchanged."[1]

This is no longer the case. Mechanization may not have led to any major change in skills required of the compositor, but solid-state electronics (transistors and semiconductors) and digitization—the currency of the electronic revolution—have. Setting type by hand in the early 1990s is the sole endeavor of the hobby printer, and his commercial counterpart, the fine-art revival printer. Most compositors now find themselves seated in front of computer terminals.

The nineteenth-century compositor handled both typesetting and composing (makeup) of a page, but the mid-to-late twentieth century brought a division of labor that would separate and transform these tasks into glorified secretarial work and cut-and-paste jobs. It is no wonder that the recent transition from hot to cold composition is felt as a drastic and categorical, if not catastrophic, change. Materials changed, processes changed, the quality of work conditions and of work produced changed, and, perhaps most important, the status of the printer changed.

The Photocomposition Era

The transmission of power in the semiautomated typecasting machines of the late nineteenth and early twentieth centuries used a mixture of manual, mechanical, and electrical energy. Type images were assembled after molten metal was cast from brass matrices. In the world of cold composition, the transmission of power in typesetting machines has progressed through stages of photomechanical, electromechanical, and electronic energy. Even during the earliest stages of development in the late 1940s, photocomposition machines were computer aided. The more electronically sophisticated they became, the more mechanical parts they shed.

In hindsight, people in the trade conceive of these computer-aided typesetting systems as successive "generations" of type composition. At the present time there are four generations to speak of, although the changes keep coming, and some specialists have given up counting. Much like losing track of how distant relatives are related, they refer to anything past the third generation as "post–third generation."

First-generation phototypesetters, such as the Harris Intertype Fotosetter and the British Monophoto, worked on the principle of reproducing type from a matrix much like their hot-metal counterpart, the Linotype, only what once was done with brass and molten metal was now done with photographic film and light. The Mergenthaler Linotype Company named this new member of its family the Linofilm. When I asked Dick Harrison what the most radical technological change in the twentieth century had been, he responded with several spoken paragraphs on photocomposition:

"I would have to say it was in the late fifties and early sixties when photocomposition came into play. That's when the real wise guys like Rocappi and John Seybold were active.[2]

"The demise of hot metal probably was around 1968, '66, somewhere in there. Manufacturers stopped making a lot of hot-metal machines. They did their best to speed the existing ones up with water-cooled casting mechanisms and that kind of thing. The Harris Fotosetter, which was the negative equivalent for the brass matrix, was an attempt to keep the old Linotype and just replace the hot-metal pot with a camera. The magazines and everything would be the same. But it required a big investment in hardware because it produced film. And then to make corrections you had to die-cut out the line and strip in a new line from a correction piece.

"And the Photon guys said, 'Well, the heck with that. I'll just start with discs and drums.' The Photon people are the people who put a big hole in the hot-metal approach. But the big Monarch casters that used to go maybe thirteen lines a minute—that was as fast as you could cast metal and have it solidify in time, drop in the galley . . ." Dick laughs at the thought, ". . . without running off the corners, you know."[3]

Ed Jacob remembers the advent of offset printing as being equipment-centered:

"Along came offset and it was different. It was the dynamic change in my time. It was never a threat till the quality went up. Then it drove hot metal right out.

"And it was primarily because the litho people had enough sense to concentrate their money and talent to develop the equipment, 'kay? A lot of letterpressmen thought that it would never succeed. And with the advent of lithography came good-quality camera work. They drove the engravers to the graveyard."[4]

Engravers were not the only ones threatened by the dynamic change in printing technology. Death was a fitting metaphor for what lay ahead, especially in a trade where tools and materials are so graphically anthropomorphized. When the protagonist in John Updike's novel *Rabbit Redux* is called into his boss's office and fired, he handles the news with morbid sarcasm. The plant is converting to offset printing. We are witness to the uncomfortable encounter between employer and employee.

> "So no linotypers, huh?"
> Pajasek looks up startled; his eyebrows arch and drop . . .
> "I thought I made that point. That's part of the technical picture, that's where the economy comes. Offset, you operate all from film, bypass hot metal entirely. Go to a cathode ray tube, Christ, it delivers two thousand lines a minute, that's the whole *Vat* in seven minutes. We can keep a few men on, retrain them to computer tape, we've worked the deal out with the union, but this is a sacrifice, Harry, from the management point of view. I'm afraid you're far down the list . . ."
> "O.K.," Rabbit says. "When do I knock off?"
> "Harry, this hurts me like hell. You learned a skill and now the bottom's dropping out. Maybe one of the Brewer dailies can take you on, maybe something in Philly or up in Allentown, though what with papers dropping out or doubling up all over the state there's something of a glut in the trade right now."
> "I'll survive. What did Kurt Schrack do?"
> "Who he?"
> "You know. The *Schockelschtuhl* guy."
> "Christ, him. That was back in B.C. As I remember he bought a farm north of here and raises chickens. If he's not dead by now."
> "Right. Die I guess would be the convenient thing. From the management point of view."[5]

All optimism is squelched; the Linotypers' days are numbered. Rabbit, himself, is headed for the hellbox, his skills a dead matter.

In the early 1960s, when computers began to enter newspaper composing rooms, there were nearly eleven thousand ITU members *past* retirement age (over 10 percent of the union's total membership) who were eligible for pensions. This situation forced the union to negotiate fringe benefits and direct payments into union funds in exchange for automation.[6]

Computers were not accepted in the composing room without a struggle. Seeking strike sympathizers, the Richmond (Virginia) Typographical Union No. 90 paid for the following copy to be broadcast on radio station WENZ:

> So you're almost sixty years old. Got a couple of grandchildren too. You've worked hard to make a go of things. Got a good job and took pride in your work. You like your job and the people you work with. Next month you'll have over forty years on the same job. And then one day, the company doesn't need you anymore. The company wants to replace you with new computers and unskilled labor. The company won't even let you learn how to operate the new computers. After all those years of hard work, you would have to start all over again. Richmond newspapers did all this to the members of the Typographical Union No. 90. If you disapprove of this kind of treatment of long-time employees, *cancel your paper and support the strike!*[7]

If Linotype operators were given the opportunity to stay on at a printing establishment that had converted to photocomposition and offset printing, they had to be prepared for a number of changes. To begin with, they had to learn the lay of an entirely new keyboard, since the one they were accustomed to on the Linotype differs from that of a standard typewriter QWERTY-lay. This constitutes a fundamental change. Printers have traditionally sought to limit the numbers admitted to their ranks by controlling apprenticeships and insisting on closed, i.e., union, shops. The mystery of their craft has been perpetuated by the continuing use of archaic terminology and the enduring practice of strange initiation rites. The setting of type "upside down and backwards," necessitated by the letterpress printing process, has meant that printers, alone, could easily decipher the jumble of metal letters locked up in forms to be printed.

Once compositors learn the keyboard of an electronic word processor, however, they relinquish sole control over the input of text. They are joined by journalists, editors, proofreaders, and advertising personnel, all of whom can input their own text and corrections on their own computer terminals, thereby bypassing the composing room altogether.

In addition to adjusting to a new keyboard-lay, and the scaled-down physical movement it requires, the former hot-metal compositor must adjust to the handling of entirely different materials, namely paper and paste.

Photocomposition is comprised of two basic processes: *input,* where the type is entered on an electronic word processor equipped with a video display terminal (VDT), and *output,* where the type is generated in material form. The product of text output is called "reproduction proof" or "repro"; it is used as "camera-ready copy" in the printing process. As it emerges from a photoprocessor, like film from a canister, the text appears on long, narrow strips of slippery paper. It must then be organized, cut, pasted or waxed, arranged, and adhered to illustration board according to a layout design. This process is called "pasteup" and results in a series of boards which comprise the future pages of a printed piece, be it a book, brochure, poster, or newspaper.

In hot-metal composing, this process of assembly was called makeup and was handled by a stonehand. When his tools and materials (lead, wood, mitres, and saws) were replaced with X-acto blades, T-squares, paper, and paste, the process was renamed "paste-makeup." In time, the phrase has been shortened to "pasteup."

The next step in prepress preparation is imposition. This involves the arrangement of pages in a rectangular formation in the final position in which they will be printed. It is the size and shape of the paper stock, and how it will be folded and gathered, that determine the exact positioning of individual pages. In metal, this work is done on a flat steel working surface (once made of stone—hence the name "stonehand"). The multiple pieces of text and display type, illustration matter, and spacing material are surrounded by furniture which provides space for the margins and holds the many individual pieces square. As mentioned earlier, a steel frame, or chase, is placed around the form and secured by quoins which wedge and expand at the corners. The process of tightening and knocking down any unsettled type is called "lockup." Recall Ed Jacob's story about locking-up the form and how important it was to "take a whack at the thing" to be sure nothing would drop when the form was lifted.

In photocomposition, pages are created on film or paper. Imposition can be accomplished at computer terminals with the aid of programs developed to combine composition and makeup, automating the process of page production. The present-day compositor and pasteup artist labor with the knowledge that system "[p]agination, or computer page makeup, is on the verge of making the entire composing room obsolete."[8]

Quality: A Disharmony of Voices

The increased speed of text output during the early transition to photocomposition was impressive, but there were problems with the reproductive quality of individual typefaces. In fact, they reproduced too well—something their creators had not accounted for when originally designing the type.

Typefaces initially designed for letterpress printing, like Hermann Zapf's Palatino and William A. Dwiggins's Caledonia, lost their punch in the offset printing process. In time, companies such as Mergenthaler, British Monotype, and the American Type Foundry worked in consultation with type designers to redesign classic typefaces in order to accommodate the new technology. A similar situation exists today where many of the old metal typefaces are being adapted for digital typesetting. The problem comes when the art of typography is left solely in the hands of electronics engineers, equipment manufacturers, and computer programmers who lack adequate understanding of type design.

Caflisch writes that, "[t]echnically speaking, offset printing provides a maximum of sharpness and is, therefore, superior to letterpress. Since, however, most of the types used in offset were originally designed for reproduction by letterpress, they appear unnaturally 'pointy' and bloodless in offset."[9] (Note the anthropomorphism toward type.) Improvements in the reproductive quality of printing took place before type design caught up to do justice to the process. Indeed, it was the invention of offset printing that created the need for photocomposition.

Remember that the third dimension, a hallmark of letterpress printing, owes its strength to the type's raised metal surface, which is designed and cut to accommodate inkspread. This three-dimensionality is lost in the transition to offset where the printing surface, generated from a phototypesetter on photosensitized paper, becomes a two-dimensional image. A more detailed explanation may help one visualize the difference.

In letterpress printing, a lot of ink and pressure are required to get a decent impression. This pressure squeezes the ink around the edges of each letterform, causing the printed letter to appear heavier and stronger than the face on the original metal type. Typographers took this ink-squeeze into account when designing their metal faces; that is, they aesthetically reduced the metal letterforms to allow for the ink-squeeze in printing. Likewise, when metal typefaces are adapted for phototypesetting and offset printing, the drawings of letterforms have to be corrected to allow for the *lack* of inkspread.

Typographical quality suffered not because of the changeover to phototypesetting and offset printing, but because of how the transition was initially handled. Greer Allen, while University Printer at Yale, offered this interpretation of the situation:

> Standards of quality always drop when the guidelines, the yardsticks, the expectations which are second nature to the experienced craftsman of the old technique, are not transferred and integrated into the fabric of the new manufacturing technology. . . .
>
> The best example is a recent one. In the evolution from hot-metal to cold-type, the engineers thought they could quietly bypass craftsmen, who for years had been planning type faces for hot-metal machines, by simply photo-copying sharp repro[duction] proofs of metal-set type on enamel paper and trans-

ferring them to film for cold-type projection, ignorant of the fact that the metal face had been designed in contemplation of image-gain in the letterpress impression.

Well in the first decades, before the new film machine companies realized their error and called in letterpress craftsmen to draw type faces especially for film, in those first decades film composition proliferated a weak, emaciated library of alphabets which are the sick heritage of us all today. [10]

Allen's comments illustrate the quintessential role that craftsmen can and must play in the continuity of quality control.

While first-generation typesetters were modeled on the hot-metal machines that preceded them, second-generation typesetters were specifically designed to set type by photomechanical means. [11] In the latter, a light source passes through a negative image of the type character from a photographic master. These images are then projected onto photosensitive film or paper.

Third-generation typesetters differ markedly in that light is not shined through a photographic master; instead, the character is generated electronically on the face of a cathode ray tube. A cathode ray tube, or CRT, is actually a small television tube that generates a line pattern similar to the one that forms a picture on a television screen. The CRT is an electronic scanning device that forms and projects type characters onto photographic film or paper. The result is used for camera-ready copy in offset printing.

In the majority of third-generation machines, the characters are stored not as analogic photographic images but in digital form. Once generated in a dot matrix pattern, the image is then photographed and can be manipulated electronically to alter the character's point size, slant, height, and width. [12] In addition to offering the aforementioned flexibility, these third-generation typesetters are fast—so fast that they are difficult to believe. Ed Jacob communicates his astonishment to me one day, as we are eating lunch:

"This is a figure that's hard to accept: fifteen thousand pages a day! That takes a battery of people to handle the output. Down at the GPO Office [Government Printing Office]—that's just one damn machine. Christ, that's mind boggling."

"And what kind of machine does that?"

"The video 80/2. It's a really powerful, high-speed machine. It's probably the only one in the country. Video draws a character with strokes . . ."

Ed sketches vertical strokes that outline a roman capital *A*, then takes a few bites from his sandwich.

"Kinda crude, but the letter *A*. When I worked at Rocappi we had a Harris Fototronic. It would draw that *A* with dots, okay? If you put a magnifying glass on it you can see, it gets a little bumpy. This is a sawtooth, you know, like the ocean. Now when you look at one letter and that whole letter is formed by dots, and you're saying twelve hundred characters *a second*, it's mind boggling to think that that damn thing can draw all these dots just for one letter and it can do twelve hundred in a second. You know?

"When I went into this field—now you know, I go back to the old-timers, and they say, 'No Goddamn way, Ed! You got your numbers wrong.' And in the times I think, my God, how—I can't grasp that technology that can do it!

"Over at the GPO, when the job was running they had a little window light proof where you could look in. And you could see the lines. You couldn't see it *as* it was set. It was *so* fast. But you could see the lines.

"It's like someone who was looking in the window, took a galley . . ." Ed suddenly swipes his hand away, hitting the edge of the table, as if pulling a galley sheet, ". . . and pulled it down. *Extremely* fast. It's the closest you could come to understanding the speed of the machine. We put a monitor up, a t.v. monitor, and like we, we set . . ." he stops midsentence realizing the mixed company ". . . an obscene word. I forget how many thousands of times. On a tape. Then we duped it. Twice that many thousands, just to get the word to sit there for a flash so you could see it. That proved how fast the machine was. You couldn't see it flicker but the word froze, because you were looking at the same word, oh, I don't know, maybe eight thousand times. So, you know, this is a little hard for the old . . ." He chuckles, ". . . the older printers to buy. Right?" [13]

While these newer machines make tremendous gains in speed and flexibility possible, they also create the potential for loss in typographic integrity. Because there is often only one original image in phototypesetting, this true-drawn character must be electronically altered, and some would say distorted, in order to generate a range of point sizes and typographic specifications, e.g., small capitals, italic, oblique, condensed, and expanded typefaces. This is particularly offensive to people with hot-metal backgrounds, like Carl Gross, who recognize that a majority of typefaces are digitized by electronic engineers who did not deal with original drawings. "They take a small master, blow it up twelve hundred times, and it goes out the window." [14]

Ed Jacob may be impressed with the new machine's speed, but he is fairly negative about its effective use:

"There has been a compromising away of quality. What screws it up is you can't design a face that will survive anamorphic expansion and reduction. Type is designed for a set width or point size. In the old typefoundries, they cut type for each size, and some beautiful printing was done in just a few sizes.

"Before the advent of this revolution, the average shop didn't have many faces. They *had* to have better design. They might have Caslon—the whole family. We used to have just even sizes—6, 8, 10, 12, 14. Then the ad men would say, 'I like it, but I need it a bit bolder, or slightly larger.' Before too long, we had odd and even point sizes and half sizes." [15]

Typographer Carl P. Rollins expresses a similar view in discussing the work of two turn-of-the-century book and type designers. An advocate of an economy of scarcity, Rollins reminds us that D. B. Updike and Bruce Rogers built their reputations on four to six typefaces. [16] The implication is that too much freedom invites mediocrity. And that mediocrity goes unnoticed by people who, unfortunately, do not know any better.

Ed Jacobs remarked, "I still feel that quality is way downhill in typesetting. But, who cares? It's like furniture—today it's made of cardboard. They *print* the grain on. People accept it." [17]

There is no doubt that photocomposition changed the face of printing forever, both literally and metaphorically. What is intriguing is the emotional investment people make in assessing its impact. There are those that vouch for its superiority, and those that lament the passing of the old ways. With quality at issue, the former faction contends that things have gotten better, while the latter argues that things have gotten worse. An early-morning conversation with union local president Bertram A. Powers made this division suddenly clear.

I asked him what he thought about the typographic quality of printing, now that photocomposition had superseded hot-metal composition. His response was automatic. "The typographic quality has gotten better."

I had heard so much to the contrary that the statement was a surprise.

I asked him, "Would the compositors think so?"

"No," he responded, and paused. "But they would be wrong." [18]

Oh. And why should I be surprised? Adherence to the old ways of doing things during transitional periods is nothing new, nor is technological change in itself. In fact, the history of printing could be told by recounting those moments when technological shifts have occurred. Whether it be the shift from scribal manuscript to movable type, from hand cut punches to mechanically engraved matrices, from hot-metal type to cold type, or from analogue to digital, *all* have involved periods of technological retooling. Those who welcome the changes tend to belittle those who do not, as if their adversity to change is indicative of a weakness in character.

Listen to this gathering of printers at an auction where hot-metal and phototypesetting equipment is being sold off. The auctioneer is halfway through the L-lot of Ludlow equipment. An older man gestures toward one of three Linotype machines that nobody is interested in buying.

Fig. 41. Auction at John C. Spencer Company, Chester, Pennsylvania, 1985. Photo by the author.

"I used to run one of those. Way back in the forties."

"Where did you work?"

"I worked for an outfit in Allentown. Then we had photo-composition."

"Do you think the quality is the same?"

"No. It's better."

"Better now?"

"Yeah, because your offset is much better printing than with your letterpress. Much, much sharper. There's no comparison. And yet you have people who insist that they want letterpress printing.

"But you cannot do as good a job on letterpress as you can with offset because you're taking the ink and you're pressing those letters and forcing them in the paper. And with the textured paper, forget it. You lose it."

"What was it like working on one of those machines?" I ask, pointing to the row of Linotypes.

"Kinda boring."

The attention returns to the wiseguy auctioneer. "There are two of them. All brass. Five dollars . . . anyone for five dollars? Ten dollars over there. Thirty-five over here. Forty over there. Forty-five I got."

The men I am standing with are not impressed with this auctioneer's style. "Gee, I think that guy is looking for a basket-ball court. Show him where it is," says Armand Montana, who runs an equipment leasing company in Allentown, Pennsylvania. He has been listening to this talk about Linotypes.

"You know, it took thirty years to get the people around those . . ." Montana gestures toward the Linotypes, ". . . to listen to you."

"What do you mean?"

"To switch. There's nothing better than this—it's the best thing since sliced bread! You know."

We laugh.

"What, the Linotype?"

Montana is incredulous. "They wouldn't change! It's the same way with offset. You know, there's a lot of printers who would say, 'You have to go letterpress. No offset, that's no good; that'll never last. Nobody'll buy it, nobody'll like it.' Then I used to show 'em stuff reduced. And they'd say, 'That looks good, but I still don't like it.'

"Yeah, old letterpress versus offset. They won't accept it. No. Like the guys that had to give up stick shifts for the automatic transmission. 'The automatics will never last,' they said."

Our attention drifts back to the auctioneer. "Anybody want the stone? Okay, next lot. T-162. Black and Decker jigsaw. Oh boy, look at that beauty. There it is, a Black and Decker jigsaw. Anybody want it?"

"I'll give you two dollars for it," someone offers.

"It's electric, mister. You're telling me two dollars for electric? You want it, Holtzberg? It'll jig for you. Press the button and it jigs." Montana continues:

"My father-in-law, when the turn signals come out, he

thought that was crazy, says, 'It's safer when you put your hand out the window.' I says, 'What happens at *night* or when it rains or it's cold outside? You don't see!' 'No,' he says, 'That's safer.' Honest to God. I had a hell of a time trying to win him over."

The thought of this stubborn in-law makes Montana chuckle. "People are averse to change." [19]

Hundreds of miles away, in another region of the United States, reactions to technological change were similar. Printer Barnie Weeks recalls union members' resistance to teletypesetters at the Montgomery, Alabama, newspaper plant where he worked. Weeks was number two or three in seniority at the time the teletypesetters were introduced.

"It was like pulling eye teeth to get them to train. We would approach members, who were Linotype operators, to begin learning the typewriter keyboard. The first position they would take was, 'It'll never work.' And when they exhausted that, 'Well, they'll never get them here.' And then when they began to bring the crates in months and months later, 'Well, it won't affect me; I've been here long enough. I've got enough seniority.'

"The union took the view that you couldn't fight technology and that you had to adapt to it. Only by improved productivity, due to technology, could you continue raising wages, bettering hours, and working conditions. By and large, 95 percent of the members were like most people that you run into on the street; *they resist change.*"[20]

Understandably so, especially when the change at hand subsumes a person's lifework. Consider the printers who apprenticed in hot-metal composing rooms. Suddenly, in mid-life, they find the ground rules of their craft undeniably altered.

"I started in 1950 as a Linotype operator in State College, Pa., and I thought I'd be set for life," says Fred Zehner, who sports a crewcut. Fred had only been at the Union Printers Home for two months when I met him. He sums up the demise of hot metal in a few short sentences. "Then they got new equipment and I had to learn to be a tape puncher on the TTS. Then they abandoned that and got a new system. And I had to learn to operate a computer! That's when I quit."[21]

Carl Schlesinger, who served a printing apprenticeship in New York City from 1947 to 1952, expresses much the same chagrin: "At the beginning of my own apprenticeship our teachers impressed us with the school's unofficial motto—Benjamin Franklin (Poor Richard's) advice: 'He that hath a trade, hath an estate.' Starting in the late 1950s, that 'trade' proved to be elusive, as we retrained two, three, and even four times in order to hold onto our trade, so we could have an 'estate.'"[22]

In addition to having to accommodate to entirely new systems, printers must accept that the tools and hard won skills of their handicraft tradition—like mortising, for instance, a hot-metal procedure—no longer have value. Dick Harrison describes what happens when the camera interlopes on a hot-metal problem:

"Here's your mortising now . . ." Just as Ed Jacob had done, Dick writes out the word "water," a demonstration standard.

"See, the letters were cut with a saw. You would cut a notch out of the *A* here and a notch out of the *W* there and then they would slide together. You would mortise in order to kern, which is moving two letters closer together.

"With photocomposition, two images can occupy the same space because it's photographic and the latent image can be piled up, one on top of the other. Whereas in hot metal, you had a physical thing, so you had to mortise the letters to do kerning."

Another technique comes to mind.

"Mitred corners on rules.[23] We don't do that today. It's just butted photographically. Square corners. But you used to have to mitre them so that they worked just like a picture frame. A mitring machine."

"So is it right to say that there has been a general shift from moving mechanical parts—"

"—And hand craftsmanship," he adds, "carpentry and lead, I call it . . ."

". . . to optics?"

"Yeah. Not only optics but tape and glue. Because you can buy rules in tape and just glue it down. I mean, it comes in a strip. You put it down and cut it with a knife. You can tape all kinds of rule borders with just plain old black Chartpak tape."[24]

Across the Atlantic Ocean, in London, newspaper compositors talk in remarkably similar ways. They too have experienced the same transition from hot metal to cold composition, involving the shift from metal to paper:

"When you are putting a 'box' round an advert for instance, a fancy rule . . . in hot metal you would have to go to a rack to find a particular rule, walk to a saw, cut the rule to length, go to a mitring machine and mitre the corners, walk back to the stone with it and fit it into the page. You may well have to put some little 'leads' down the side to get it to fit correctly. Compare that with paper make-up: you have a box full of rolls of Chartpak plastic strip beside you. You peel some off, stick it on the page and knife off the spare. About 15 seconds, I should think, compared with two minutes."[25]

Dick Harrison's discussion of the lost art of mitring and mortising moved him to speak about the changing role of the printer. "There's a loss of, I quote, 'traditional craft,' in the production of the stuff today because it's so less labor intensive, and anyone can get involved. So there's no legend. There's no aura to being a printer anymore. Like Ben Franklin said, 'Ben Franklin, *Printer.*'"[26]

Dick is referring to Franklin's epitaph, which any self-respecting printer knows by heart. "The highest tribute ever paid to the printer's craft was expressed in three words by one of the world's greatest minds, who, in writing his own epitaph, put aside his triumphs as scientist, philosopher, reformer, and diplomat, and began: I, Benjamin Franklin, Printer . . ."[27]

Dick continues to speak about printing in Franklin's day. "In those days, [printing] was something. Like a teacher—go to Europe, a teacher is a very revered person, and so is a soldier. But not so here. A teacher? He can't *do* anything else. And everybody associates printers with the speedy print shops, the Xeroxes.

"You know, you don't see tapestries being done anymore either today. Bead weaving? That's gone. Nobody here makes baskets, you buy them from Taiwan."[28]

The real heart of the matter is that men have been displaced by machines. There simply is no longer a need for many of the skills that once defined a printer; for example, the make-ready process in letterpress printing. Ed Jacob recalls the special skills of the Bible printers who worked with very fine paper.

"I think the most difficult job that I know of was Bible printers, because they use small type but they also handle such fine paper. See, [in letterpress] you're printing from a raised surface, not an offset plate. So some of the type might be sticking up too high or too low while the cylinder, which was like a heavy, waxed parchment, would cover it. They'd take that paper back—ach . . ."

"Need a pen? Here." Ed accepts my felt-tip pen and begins to draw.

"Okay, that's your type. Now here's the cylinder, which of course rolls. Now, let's say this spot hits this spot. Well if that type is too low, he peels back this big sheet, he puts a little paper in, a scrap! It could be one layer you know, it depends on how far you've got. He puts a little tissue in there and then brings it back again, raising the surface to compensate for the low type.

"On the other hand, if you have something up a little high, it certainly wouldn't be that bad, that it would punch through the paper, but it would *splat* ink, see. Sometimes this would take days in a Bible house, to make-ready for a large press. This was a real skill."

"If the type was too high—"

"High or low."

". . . how would they compensate for that?" I ask Ed.

"Cut out. Or they may have to open up the chase. There might be a speck of dirt under there. When they locked it up, it kept [the dirt] out. 'Cause, you know, the ink gets coated and as

Fig. 42. Miehle letterpress ready to roll. Photo by the author.

you start running, if you add papers in here to letterspace, or a slug, the damn thing starts to work up, if that's not properly locked up. That's gone.

"There's no need for that letterpress anymore. And it would run slow because you can't run manifold paper fast." He smiles. "You know, it will start floating off into the room, Bible paper."[29]

Bob Culp also talked about the thin tissues used in make-ready work. In recounting the pressman's skill, he uses the past tense. "They would spend hours making fine adjustments. To a sixteenth of an inch. When they got through, that was a work of art. They had pride in their work."[30]

Dick Harrison calls attention to the compositor's skills with mitre and saw, additional skills that are no longer needed. "There used to be an apprenticeship for a craft and a guild and a union. The attrition rate is pretty high now. It's a natural selection process. We don't need people who can carve lead borders anymore and make the mitre, justify lines in a chase or a stick. We don't need it anymore. It's too much work."[31] Dick's associate, Ed Jacob, had come to the same conclusion. "It's not the hand quality that's gone, but the need for it."[32]

Although Dick finds fault with the conditions that have contributed to the printers' drop in status, he is more than happy to keep things the way they are. Speaking as someone who is comfortably employed in the new technology, he confesses, "[Hot metal] is fun as a hobby or as a study in the old Williamsburg-type thing where you want to say, 'Gee, this is the way they used to do it.' But heck, I wouldn't want to be pulling on a Weaver Press. Really. And I wouldn't want to be composing out of a type-case either. Not when I can sit down at a keyboard and bang out pages in minutes rather than in lines and hours."[33]

The same rhetoric existed in print more than half a century earlier, in an *Inland Printer* article entitled "The Good Old Days that Never Were." Instead of comparing cold type to hot, the writer contrasts hot type with handset: "The Linotype operator misses some of the fun of the old hand-set days, but he wouldn't swap for them half as eagerly as the old-timers would have swapped for the machine."[34]

Who can say? With hindsight comes the hazards of presentism. The fact is that Dick Harrison holds a managerial position in the new technological environment. Not everybody fared equally well in the cold-composition climate. Retraining has recast Linotype operators as keyboard typists and stonemen as pasteup "artists." The new roles demand a relinquishing of power; the crafts people's loss is the managers' gain.

Cynthia Cockburn discusses the transfer in power that accompanied the shift from metal to paper:

> Lead alloy and the machinery used to process type may have literally belonged to the capitalist, but in effect they belonged to the compositor, who alone knew how to put them to work. Paper and glue—these are materials of the kindergarten. . . . The journalists and editors who come down to the stone to see their stories being made up used to be unable to read the lead type except with difficulty, back to front as it was. Now they look over the comp's shoulder and can read the bromides as well as he. Composing has lost its mystique and the compositor much of his authority. He no longer has to interpret or explain, he can no longer blind the editors with technical knowhow.[35]

The experience, sentiment, and testimony of British and American compositors is strikingly similar. Former hot-metal compositors turned pasteup hands, employed in the London printing trade, complain: "Executive desk, that's the name they give one of these jobs. Sounds grand, doesn't it? But I could give that job to my seven-year-old daughter. As for putting bromides through the waxer, a toddler could do it. Nothing could be more soul-destroying. . . . It was always a useful psychological barrier between you and the editor, that piece of metal. . . ."[36]

The switch to cold type at the *New York Times* affected makeup compositor Arthur George in an equally negative fashion: "To me it's no challenge anymore. Editors used to come up and work with you. 'Does this fit? Can we make this work?' You had a sense of artistry. You were a craftsman. Now you paste it on the board. There's nothing to it."[37] Dan Burns, known for his skill at makeup composition, expresses the same disheartening thought in these words: "When I was young, even before my time, printers used to wear high hats. They were supposed to be *artists*. Today it's nothing. Today it's all machine stuff."[38]

Compare the locking up of a form of hot-metal slugs and

wood furniture to composing type by keyboarding at a computer terminal. The former was often dangerous and dirty work, requiring substantial physical strength. It was active, purposeful, and concrete in character. In comparison, the latter is relatively hygienic, immaterial, abstract, and inactive work. Although fatiguing, it does not require great physical strength.

The printers' use of language is ironically accurate. For a hot-metal compositor, type was either dead or alive. For a computer keyboarder, typematter is neither alive nor dead, but truly resurrectable at the mere stroke of a key. This is the cold-composition working environment. Clean, quiet, no burning lead, no oppressive heat.

Notes

1. A. J. M. Sykes, "The Cohesion of a Trade Union Workshop Organization," *Sociology* 1, no. 1 (1967): 147. It should be noted that Sykes is writing about the printing industry in Great Britain.

2. Harrison remembers Rocappi as an individual when in fact it is the name of a pioneering computer-composition service bureau started by John Seybold in the early 1960s. Rocappi is an acronym standing for Research on Computer Application in the Printing and Publishing Industry.

3. Dick Harrison, tape-recorded interview, 23 November 1983.

4. Ed Jacob, tape-recorded interview, 30 November 1983.

5. John Updike, *Rabbit Redux,* 297–98.

6. Smith, *Goodbye Gutenberg,* 227.

7. WENZ, Richmond, Virginia, radio script, undated. Used with permission, Georgia State University, Special Collections.

8. Andrew Zimbalist, "Technology and the Labor Process in the Printing Industry," in *Case Studies on the Labor Process,* 111.

9. Max Caflisch, "On Type," *Fine Print* 9, no. 4 (October 1983): 140.

10. Greer Allen, "How the Craftsmen Face Change," interview in *Inland Printer,* March 1976, 108.

11. Seybold, *World of Digital Typesetting,* 112.

12. Ibid., 72–74, and 112–13.

13. Ed Jacob, tape-recorded interview, 30 November 1983.

14. Carl Gross, personal communication, November 1983.

15. Ed Jacob, tape-recorded interview, 30 November 1983.

16. Rollins, *Off the Dead Bank,* 52.

17. Ed Jacob, tape-recorded interview, 30 November 1983.

18. Bertram Powers, interview, 1 November 1985.

19. This exchange took place during a public auction held at the John C. Spencer Company, 11 December 1985. The printing plant, located in Chester, Pennsylvania, had been in business since the Civil War.

20. Barnie Weeks, tape-recorded interview in Montgomery, Alabama, 12 December 1988.

21. Fred Zehner, New York No. 6. Tape-recorded conversation during a birthday party at the Union Printers Home, 3 February 1988.

22. Carl Schlesinger, personal communication, February 1990.

23. Rules are lines of unvarying width (although some rules swell in the center). They can be used to create boxed areas and to separate text or illustrative material. Sometimes they serve a purely decorative purpose.

24. Dick Harrison, tape-recorded interview, 23 November 1985.

25. British newspaper compositor quoted in Cockburn, *Brothers,* 105

26. Dick Harrison, tape-recorded interview, 23 November 1985.

27. *Inland Printer* 75 (May 1925). See also, Carl Van Doren, *Benjamin Franklin* (New York: Book-of-the-Month-Club, Inc., 1980), 124.

28. Dick Harrison, tape-recorded interview, 23 November 1985.

29. Ed Jacob, tape-recorded interview, 30 November 1985.

30. Bob Culp, told to me during work, 21 June 1985.

31. Dick Harrison, tape-recorded interview, 23 November 1985.

32. Ed Jacob, tape-recorded interview, 30 November 1985.

33. Dick Harrison, tape-recorded interview, 23 November 1985.

34. Edward N. Teall, "The Good Old Days that Never Were," *Inland Printer* 75 (November 1925): 260–61.

35. Cockburn, *Brothers,* 197. A bromide is the British equivalent of reproduction proofs.

36. Quoted in Cockburn, *Brothers,* 105.

37. Makeup compositor quoted in Carey Winfrey, "The Times Enters a New Era of Electronic Printing: How It Was, How It Is," *New York Times,* 3 July 1978, 21 and 28.

38. Dan Burns, tape-recorded interview, 13 September 1985.

6

From Specialist to Paperhanger: The Printer's Status

One morning, a few years ago, I hurried along a downtown street in Philadelphia. The usual display of storefront signage competed for pedestrian attention: dry cleaners, audio equipment, women's apparel, typewriter repair, parking garage. One sign caught my eye—two lines of ersatz, Gothic bold lettering on white plexiglass:

> Ye Olde Print Shop
> Quik Offset Printing.

The spirit of tradition coupled with the expedience of modernity was the intended message, and as credible as a fast-food chain's use of "country fresh, old-fashioned cookin'." Speed and quality vie for position in the advertising rhetoric of the present. In the rhetoric of the hot metal tradition there was no question of which came first, as criteria of production and service. The contrast between the two eras, from the printer's point of view, is summed up here by Dan Burns:

"In hot metal—I used to enjoy getting a final result on something. I think things had to be more accurate then than they are now. Now, they're looking for speed. We didn't work on speed; we worked on quality. Now there are a lot of things going on that you'd never get away with." [1]

Joe Malady, one of the younger residents at the Printers Home, expressed the same frustration with speed over quality:

"When the printer had a job to do, he did it to the best of

his ability. And he stood back and took some pride in it. But today, it's more commercial. What the hell if it isn't spelled right, they know what we mean.

"It's like everything else—bang, bang, bang, get it out. Take the money and run."[2]

Ed Jacob voiced an epigram which sums up the impossibility of pleasing customer expectations in an age of fast service: "Quality, price, speed. Pick any two."

In the preceding chapters, through description and the talk of printers, I have tried to portray what work was like in hot metal. Time has passed and this is no longer an accurate description of the way things are generally done. With the exception of Heritage Printers in North Carolina, the portrayal of the hot-metal world stands as a reconstruction of conditions and experience, shaped by individual and collective memory. What of a present-day observation, and subsequent description of how phototypesetting and offset printing are done? Both are subject to a similar process of traditionalizing the present, for any description, past, present, or future, is an imaginative construction. What we observe and interpret is affected by our previous experience and what it has taught us to "see." My glimpse into the current state of affairs stems from research, and from holding various positions in printing and publishing. It is also influenced greatly by my knowledge and respect for what came before. I, like the printers who weathered the change, judge the world on the basis of cumulative experience.

Part of my on-the-job observation included periodic visits to printing plants. These planned events turned out to be packaged tours—selective, intentional, and rehearsed. Led by management, they were as representative of the actual working environment as any public-relations material is. Yet the tours were useful as indicators of the image a company wished to portray to the public. I have been on four such tours of large typesetting and printing establishments: Baum Printing Company located in northeast Philadelphia; Graphic Arts Composition and Packard Press, both downtown Philadelphia firms; and Meriden-Stinehour Press of

Meriden, Connecticut.[3] In addition, I benefitted from three more individualized tours of smaller typesetting houses: Deputy Crown of Camden, New Jersey; G & S Typesetters of Austin, Texas; and Heritage Printers of Charlotte, North Carolina. On two of the latter, I went as a representative of a university press, that is, as a client.

The substantive and structural similarity among these seven plant tours is not surprising, considering that they are designed to be informative and impressive. After all, they are largely intended to satisfy and dazzle a paying clientele, in a buyer's market. To quote writer Beatrice Warde: "Printing is still commissioned: which means that maker and buyer still have to reach their respective notions of what the job will be worth to them, before the making can start; . . . The conversations and trial-pages which precede the weeks of actual production keep alive a spirit of mutual respect and collaboration which is more than five hundred years old."[4]

Once the job is in production, *le client est roi*, or so he or she is led to believe at some of the larger commercial printers, while accommodated in interior-designed rooms. Printing plants, such as Packard and Baum in Philadelphia, boast gracious conference areas complete with executive gratuities such as a full bar, plush-covered furniture, giant video screens, framed "art," and access to rooftop tennis courts or other fitness facilities. The luxury conference rooms serve a mercenary purpose, somewhat like the complimentary drinks offered by gambling casinos. One sales representative was divulging no secrets when he told us, "We have conference rooms. Lawyers stay all night and spend thousands making revisions—which we're glad to accommodate."

A Modern-Day Printer: Packard Press

I joined the tour of Packard Press somewhat as an outsider. Karen Gaines, editor of *Almanac*, the University of Pennsylvania's faculty newsletter, had mentioned that I was welcome to join staff members and work-study students on their trip to Packard, a commercial printer that supplied them with the bulk of their typesetting and printing needs. Sales Representative Ken Henry led the tour, taking us through a number of work areas: executive wing, composition room, prepress preparation department, pressroom, and bindery.

Packard Press has adopted the classic Packard touring sedan as a symbol of the "tradition of excellence." Karen Gaines described Packard Press as a commercial printer that specializes in financial and legal work, mostly fast turnover work. We wait for all three carloads of people to arrive and then go in together as a group of twelve. Tight security measures confront the visitor: Three closed-circuit televisions, a sign-in clipboard, and a uniformed security man on duty. Three flags: city, state, and nation. Three shifts—some people are just coming in at 3:45 P.M. to start their day's work.

The Executive Suite

We begin our tour with Michael Parker, whose official title is Job Coordinator. He leads us into the executive conference room where we are introduced to Ken Henry and a barrage of flashy promotional material, including a boxed "Chromatic Pen." Henry has been with the company eight years. Until recently he was in production. He delivers the sales-rep line: As a primarily financial printer, Packard's profile has gone from a $7.5 million business in 1976 to a $35 million business in 1984. Most of their runs are medium or short. They work three complete shifts, twenty-four hours a day. Quality control. State-of-the-art equipment. Henry explains, "The new Opti-copy eliminates the imposition man and the stripper; it does in one film page what it would take five men to do. We just installed a 'Zi-Vision,' which does pagination on screen. It can format; there's no pasteup involved."

After praising the advantages of these new technological wizards he notes some drawbacks, for example, client use of word processing computers. This eliminates authors alterations [AAs], which are a source of income for the printer.

"We liked it the other way but we're gonna grow with it. If its coming, Packard will be there first."

I suddenly feel like I am in an advertisement. Henry's speech continues. He seems as programmed as the equipment he is describing:

"We are a service company. We have multiples of everything—we can't afford a breakdown. We have three web presses, three large sheet feeds, and three cameras. And a sister shop in Marlton, New Jersey."

On cue, we all rise from the oval wood-grained formica conference table and file out of the room. The carpeted corridor empties out onto a beehive of partitioned niches that are created with interior-decorator modular office furniture. The office space looks like a set from a daytime soap opera; wall-to-wall carpeting, hotel-room framed prints in soft shades, ceramic vases with silk flowers, women in high heels and dresses that rustle, men in pleated flannel pants and pastel dress shirts, lots of jewelry. We pass through this area without stopping. It is self-explanatory.

The Composition Department

The composition department consists of a number of different work areas that seem to be defined by the nature of equipment housed therein. One area is actually glassed in. It is called the "computer room" by those in its vicinity. Like the closed stack of a library, or the vault of a bank, the real treasures are kept here: the Atex 8000 computer system. Air quality and temperature are controlled. Henry boasts, "We have to keep updating our typesetting equipment to remain state-of-the-art."

Outside this room is a bank of computer terminals. A number of software designers work at them, developing programs. There is a large Linotron system and some sort of photostat machine. Six people are employed as proofreaders. Henry explains that they used to have twenty pasteup people. Now there are six. The others have become keyboard operators and proofreaders. Theirs is a union shop which means they only hire journeymen.

This is true for the typography and printing-related jobs. The executive, clerical, and sales jobs, however, are nonunion.

It is a mixed shop but something of a family shop. "A lot of fathers and sons, mothers and daughters work here and have for years." There are a number of deaf people, as there traditionally have been in the printing trade. They would seem to work at an advantage, considering the high noise level pervading the room. Minorities and handicapped workers are mentioned. "It works for us." All told, there are 450 people presently employed at the plant.

We hear something about the Zi-Vision system which handles the entire pasteup process, that is, the design and layout of text and illustrative material. The typesetters keyboard this information, and a person who is considered a program specialist types in the position. "You can pull a proof *before* you go to film!" Henry pronounces. I notice the somewhat anachronistic use of the phrase "pull a proof" for a process that no longer involves that physical action on a proof press.

The division of labor is reflected in the dress of the employees. The salaried people—customer service, sales, administration—dress more formally whereas the hourly wage people, who are union, dress more casually—shirt sleeves rolled up, ready to "get their hands dirty," even though composing is no longer a dirty business. Packard got rid of its Linotype machines five or six years ago. Dick, the foreman and floor manager, walks around with a pica ruler sticking out of his back trouser pocket. Michael Parker says that Dick has taught him a lot.

One of the programmers is working at a video display terminal, the input end of the third-generation typesetters. I ask him what he is doing and what it is called. It is not typesetting, it is formatting. We talk about the great number of typefaces and variety of sizes that are available today. He adds, with the excitement of one comfortable with limitless possibilities, ". . . and you can computer enhance whatever you've got." I cannot help but think of Ed Jacob, Carl Gross, and the generation of gentlemen typographers who would consider "enhance" a euphemism. Too much freedom can play havoc with the aesthetic standards that have been upheld by those working within the limits of traditional technology, they would say.

Henry offers a layman's description of the Linotron, a rather imposing bulk of equipment we are surrounding: "It takes commands from the computer and produces hard copy, that is, camera-ready copy. We have twenty or thirty typefonts on film. A laser beam transfers light through a mirror onto light-sensitive paper. . . ."

We leave the composition room, which is busy, noisy, full of people doing different types of jobs, and head for the second floor.

The Prepress Preparation Department

The prepress preparation department is relatively quiet. There is a noticeable chemical odor and the sound of "beautiful music" in the air. We gather around the Opti-Copy camera, which has a room of its own. Ken Henry gives a somewhat technical explanation of what it can do and then says, "The machine automatically puts pages in the order they have to be in, and then shoots them that way. It basically does the job of a stripper and an imposer."

If a VDT keyboarder once displaced the Linotype operator (who cast and assembled type), and the pasteup artist and the stripper have displaced the stonehand (who imposed, i.e., organized composed type into page forms), now it is these jobs which are being threatened by the Opti-Copy camera.

A century ago, it was the Linotype that threatened jobs. In 1891 a letter to the editor appeared in the *Inland Printer* discussing the effect of typesetting machines on working compositors. The message of the editorial was to dispel the comps' fears by concentrating on the machine's limits:

"The [typesetting] machine will never be made to set display advertisements nor job forms; nor will it in the next *thousand years* [emphasis added] be able to set even straight matter complete, without the assistance of the compositor, that is, to 'justify' the lines, correct errors and make the matter absolutely ready for the forms.

"In short, the occupation of the compositor is, in my humble opinion, improving in aspect, and it will never wane until they *get to making machinery with brains in it*" [emphasis added].[5]

Try a *hundred* years. It is 1984 and we are standing in the presence of such a machine. When Ken Henry speaks about the larger-than-life capabilities of the Opti-Copy, he anthropomorphizes its functions. "The machine tells the board how to move and what format to put the pages in. It feeds information to the camera. It's been figured out once for each size signature and page count. It saves time."

And money. What it loses are jobs. In this case, those of five men. Programming of these machines requires a machinist-craftsman to use his expertise and knowledge to translate blueprints into computer commands. Once that is done, it is more cost-efficient to run the computer. Paul K. Wright, mechanical engineer at Carnegie-Mellon University, talks about an idealized system for machining. It sounds indeed like a machine with brains in it: "An expert system is a computer program which contains all of the geometrical knowledge and all of the material knowledge, plus all of this craftsman knowledge. . . . But once we have all of those rules of thumb that these craftsmen have built up for many years, also embodied in electronic form, then we'll be able to do this unmanned machining much more easily."[6] With this kind of talk, it is easy to see the employee as a victim of management's progress.

In Cynthia Cockburn's book on craft workers and technological change, the men perceive electronic photocomposition as a threat to craft control. A proofreader gestures toward some new hardware and admits, "It's their [management's] tool, you know. And it tends to have more command over you than your pen did." In Cockburn's view, the men feel helpless in the face of capitalist authority. She quotes them as saying, "We are *victims* of progress," "we are *victims* of change."[7]

In lieu of such sentiment it is important to remember that technology, itself, is not the problem, it is what technology is made to do. A research associate at MIT has explained, "If the technology is going to victimize people, they're going to fight against it. They're not fighting against technology. They're fighting against something that victimizes them."[8]

At Packard, the Opti-Copy has exhausted our interest and Ken Henry leads the way on to the next attraction. Stepping back from the rest of the tour group, I look around at the walls, the lighting, the equipment, and the employees, a mix of young and old. I notice the absence of any pinups, which habitually decorate the walls of prepress departments, and I wonder. Women employees? Public tours? Next door in the platemaking room, sequestered from mainstream traffic, three strippers are at work cutting in negatives of illustrations for imposition.[9] Above one fellow's drafting table a large sign in red Helvetica bold warns, "Caution, Stripper at Work."

The adjacent rooms hold three generations of cameras, the Robertson being the oldest and the Opti-Copy representing the state of the art. Other names are stamped out in the grey and red metallic graphic lettering of another era, "Nuarc Plate Maker," "Flip-Top Plate Maker." Though the Opti-Copy eliminates hand-processed stripping and imposition, some jobs still have to be hand stripped, such as multicolor jobs. The Opti-Copy is good for book work and other one-color printing jobs. In this department, we are told, there are fewer people now. The machine does the job.

The Pressroom

We leave the prepress department and take the elevator to the pressroom floor—the noisiest of all. An Itek press is the first piece of equipment we see and we stop to talk about it. It has the ability to go from original copy to the printing plate and is basically used for short-run work, small runs up to a thousand. The operator explains that at one point they brought a 9500 into the pressroom and were using it to print jobs. The union said, "No way! You are taking printing jobs away from the union," and they got rid of it. "We only use the Itek for proofing jobs," an employee concedes.

The noise level is distracting to the outsider. To those working, it means business as usual—you might say, run of the press. The sound is an acoustic mix of the mechanical clack of multiple presses running and the transmitted sounds from the intercom system and individual radios. I notice a mix of men and women. Karen Gaines tells us that the women are employed in the bindery, in the trafficking of proof, in clerical jobs, and in typesetting, that is, keyboarding. Having been tangentially involved in the printing trade for years herself, she knows well enough that "the union doesn't have presswomen. The pressmen may take home $25,000 a year [in 1984]. They may never see their children. It's a personal economy built on overtime and time and a half." [10]

In publicity photographs pressmen are always pictured in short sleeves and in action, either reaching up to adjust a knob or crouching down to pull a lever. In real life, they give the impression of being "real men." This is the dirty, physically demanding, and most dangerous end of the printing business. The ones with the missing fingers are always the pressmen. Maimed hands become emblems of craftsmanship.

It is not surprising that the young pressmen in Halper's fictionalized foundry are characterized as cocksure: "The apprentices from the pressrooms stood the boldest, for they worked near dangerous machines and took chances with their limbs and fingers. They stood the cockiest. Their shirtsleeves, torn off at the armpits to prevent their arms being drawn into the machinery while they were oiling, revealed their huskiness. . . . The composing room lads, not to be out done . . . rolled their own sleeves up as high as they could go, showing that they too had biceps of a fashion." [11]

Jim Spurlock and Frank Koncel describe the pressroom at the *Chicago Tribune:* "On your big cylinder presses, those big rolls of papers going like that," Jim circles his right arm, "boy, they created a lot of static electricity, the way that thing's going around and round and round. If you happen to put your finger in there— wham! You'd be sitting on your rearend."

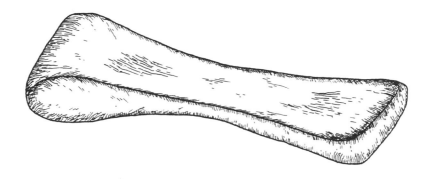

Fig. 43. Paper-folding tool in bindery. Drawn by the author.

Frank adds, "If you had fillings in your teeth, you could feel all the electricity in them. Walk underneath the row, and your hair would stand up."[12]

The pressroom at Packard Press is one very large, undifferentiated open space. There is a full range of web and sheet-fed presses. We congregate around one as Ken Henry delivers a typical sales pitch. "Fourteen thousand pages in one revolution. That's the way we do business. It's fast. It's cheap. It's effective." We move on. I notice a small wooden tool that reminds me of the "bones" used in a hot-metal shop for the folding of paper. It is resting on a protrusion below a large stack of printed stock. Henry explains: "It makes the paper flush. You use it to smooth out the paper. It came with the machine." He then adds, as if I am making too big a deal over the wooden item, "It's just a tool. I usually use a block of wood."

The Bindery

The last area we are taken through at Packard is the bindery. It is not actually physically partitioned from the pressroom. Assembly work takes place here; signatures, which are printed sheets that have been folded, are stapled or stitched together. One woman's job is to operate a mechanical hole-puncher. Another's is to feed the signatures onto a conveyor belt. I am suddenly aware of where I am. *This* is assembly-line work and these are real people doing what appear to be highly repetitive, nonskilled, robotic tasks. The impression I have gotten through the years is that bindery work (folding, trimming, collating, stapling, stitching, binding, shrink-wrapping) ranks as low-status work. And who do I see employed here? Two white women, one black woman, two black men, and one older white man.

I am overwhelmed and confused. How can I be critical of machines taking over humans' jobs and then be upset at the sight of people doing dehumanizing jobs that machines could do? Technological unemployment has robbed skilled craftspeople of their work, while leaving the less fulfilling jobs unjeopardized.[13]

The Aura of the Old-Style Printer

Bob Culp thought I was wasting my time on the tours of large printing plants. "They're more for speed. What you want is to get into a small shop where a man is using his head, eyes, and hands. But there aren't many of them left." The refrain, by now, was a familiar one.

The contrast between Packard Press and Bob's evocation of a small hot-metal print shop is indicative of a more general contrast that exists between perceptions of the current-day service establishments we are all familiar with—Sears automotive centers, PIP Instant Printing, McDonald's restaurants, K-Mart department stores—and the popular concept of their forerunners—the old-style print shop, the corner garage, the family-run restaurant, the local hardware store, the mom-and-pop candy shop. The latter have taken on legendary qualities.

What is at stake here? Scale? Familiarity? Community? Nostalgia? Raymond Williams addresses just this issue of contrast between an imagined past (rural) and experienced present (urban) in his book *The Country and the City.* Using the literature of his native England, he finds significance in the fact that the common image of the country has become an image of the past, and the common image of the city that of the future: "The pull of the idea of the country is towards old ways, human ways, natural ways. The pull of the idea of the city is towards progress, modernization, development." Often, Williams notes, the idea of the country evokes not only local memories of a rural past and the ideally shared communal memory, but the very *feel* of childhood, which we are all distanced and separated from, in the course of growing up. Enough time has passed in the history of city living to generate memories and stories about old urban working-class communities—"the delights of corner-shops, gas lamps, horsecabs, trams, piestalls: all gone"—which have the same real emotional substance as the "brooks, commons, hedges, cottages, festivals of the rural scene."

Williams regards these memoirs as invaluable, not so much for their historical accuracy but as indices of a historically grounded, shared consciousness, what he calls the "structure of feeling." "It is not so much the old village or the old back street that is significant. It is the perception and affirmation of a world in which one is not necessarily a stranger and an agent, but can be a member, a discoverer, in a shared source of life." [14]

"Perception and affirmation of a world" are what we encounter in examining the testimony of hot-metal printers. The narrative juxtapositions of the present day to a valued past of small-scale, face-to-face interactions, by people who feel they have been denied such ways of being, affirm the existence of a shared world.

Perhaps what best characterized old-fashioned service establishments was the absence of intermediary "customer service" personnel. In former times, a customer went into the type shop, or the car garage, and talked face-to-face with the printer or the mechanic. Take the typical garage with its craftsman-mechanic. He might have been a gruff, cigar-smoking, grease-under-the-fingernails character but the customer was solicitous of his skills, knowing he or she would benefit from his craftsmanship and expertise.

With today's innumerable services for household, automotive, business, and leisure needs, the market seems flooded with noncraft competitors. In order to replace the confidence once instilled by skilled shopworkers, sales personnel are forced to peddle their work and coddle their customers. In the case of a car garage, the intermediary sales force is complemented by a mediating area between street and garage; here customers are made comfortable with piped-in Muzak, brewed coffee, and a place to sit in an atmosphere free from the dirt and noise of automotive repair. One writer refers to this as the "professionalization of repair" where people are trained in schools and certified by degrees, rather than through life experience under the guidance of a master craftsman.[15]

One thing the craftsman has lost is direct contact with the client, and the satisfaction that contact can bring. The typesetting keyboarder or pasteup artist usually does not get to speak directly with the client but is bypassed by a customer service person (who may not understand all aspects of printing). Most of the talking between clients and sales people is done in a sterile environment, or over the telephone. During our tour of Packard, we never talked to anyone involved in *doing* anything; our primary contact was with sales representatives.

And what of craftsmanship, decision making, and quality? In today's economy of built-in obsolescence, it is often easier and cheaper to replace the part than repair it. Not only is the craftsman denied the opportunity to ply his tinkering ingenuity, he is often forced to relinquish the design and production decisions that once defined his role as a craftsman.

In the case of a typical old-style print shop, the customer depended on the printer's knowledge and advice as a specialist. Dick Harrison discusses the contrast between what was once the traditional domain of the shop printer, and what typifies print services today:

"In the old days, the people who needed something printed said, 'I just need a flyer' or a menu or whatever, and they would leave the design and the spelling and the form—what it looked like—to the printer. But with today's variety of garbage typefaces and variations on a theme, and your electronic anamorphic warping of typefaces, it's really a corruption of the craft. And the craftsmanship is gone; that's the part that is dying."

Dick continues to draw the contrast between then and now; it is not a promising picture:

"In the past the printer was a specialist. You abdicated all responsibility to him to do it right. A newspaper editor has the right to edit, but dare you edit art? Used to be, a printer did all. You didn't need to tell him what [type]face to use. You would no more tell him what point size to use as much as you'd tell a carpenter what tool to use for the job.

"Nowadays, it's all different. A carpenter? Today he's nothing but a hatchet man. A stonemason? He's nothing but a cinderblock man. It's the only way you can survive." [16]

Allen Byrne, now in his eighties, grew up in a printing family. He served his union apprenticeship in the 1920s and spent eight years as a tramp printer, before becoming the editor of his own hometown West Virginia newspaper. He, too, laments the printer's loss of working knowledge: "Nobody really knows his job as well as on the old [news]papers. Nobody now is a specialist the way we used to be. There used to be a foreman who supervised everyone else, but each man knew his own job to perfection. Now there is no apprenticeship, so there's a widespread lack of experience." [17]

Testimony concerning the printer's drop in status and overall competence is heard not only among the ranks of employed and retired printers, but in the writings of industrial sociologists and labor historians. [18] Comparatively well paid as tradesmen, long associated with literacy and effective union organization, the once revered aristocracy of labor has fallen from its high post. [19] The occupational status of printers is in jeopardy. Forced to abandon traditional tools and techniques, they have accommodated to cold composition, but their age-old craft identity has been shaken. In many cases, emotional statements concerning what constitutes a printer revolve around the hot/cold distinction. Retired stonehand

Dan Burns associates hot metal with quality and cold metal with speed. From his perspective, the ability to do paste makeup does not qualify one as a printer:

"There's nothing wrong with paste makeup, but to me it's not like setting type. It's sloppy, as far as I'm concerned. To me, it's . . . you're not really a printer. You're more like a paperhanger or something." Having said this, he gathers strength fed by prideful indignation. "To me, you're not a real printer."

"What would be a real printer?" I ask, recalling the words of a tramp printer a century earlier, who chose to give up the trade rather than adapt to the new typecasting machines, which in his opinion would render him more of a piano player than a typesetter.

"Getting a piece of copy, knowing what size type to use. Putting it together. Making a nice-looking job out of it and all that. Getting a final result on something, using your own head. *That's* a printer. Here, you're getting this stuff all in pieces, putting it in there.

"I don't know. I like the old way better. You could make corrections in the type by hand and all. With paste makeup, you get the stuff that's given to you and you put it in. The stuff is done on paper—they cut out parts and put them in like that, but not type. Then they photograph that, make a negative of it. That's the way it is now. When I was setting type, *we* did that." [20]

What has changed is the individual craftsman's control over the entire work process. When Bertram Powers spoke of the hot-metal world he said, "You were working with your hands. And you worked with each other; brothers—you had to work together. The Linotype man handed hard copy to the handman. You had something to do with the entire project. Not so now." [21]

For Dan Burns, the business of composing type means applying knowledge of the whole process, *making decisions about typeface, type size, and placement, making corrections on your own work, and seeing the job through* from the founding and forming of source materials to the face-to-face exchange with a paying client. Such all-inclusive activity is what characterizes traditional craft, which printing may no longer be.

"So that doesn't bode very well for the printers' trade," I suggest to Dan.

"No. But it's there. The employers even try to do away with paste makeup—try to take it out of the union. They say, even a high school girl can do it, you know? See what I mean? All you have to do is know how to place things. That's not real typography."[22]

Dan's lack of enthusiasm for what the printer's trade has become is shared by union printers in California. A questionnaire designed to elicit printers' attitudes toward technological change and employment outlook was distributed to ITU members in the late 1970s. Less than 20 percent of the 170 respondents had faith in the popular belief that "in the long run, technological change will create more jobs." Eighty-five percent believed that the future of printing appeared gloomy. One printer foresaw the end of printing altogether: "Just as blacksmiths disappeared or became mechanics with the advent of the automobile, printers will have to become electronic technicians or editor-proofreaders—whatever their personal bent dictates—if they remain with the newspapers. The very word 'print' has lost its meaning. That is not what one does to produce newspapers or job work any more."[23]

That this dismayed printer elects to speak of lost meaning rather than changed meaning in his statement about the word "print" is telling. Change does not necessarily imply loss, but loss implies change and a good bit more. That a way of life is perceived to be lost and not merely changed suggests impoverishment, involuntary compliance, and a degree of regret. For these printers, the invoking of a happier past—a world of meaning now lost—is not merely a nostalgic gesture, romanticizing the remembrance of times past. It represents a shared belief-system among craftsmen who have lived through technological change in its actual consequences and are now faced with a world in which much *has* lost its meaning: occupational jargon, training, skills, tools, materials, indeed most of what defined them as journeymen members of their trade.

It is not only the printer who finds the present system unsatisfactory. From at least one client's perspective, cold composition has its drawbacks. Stanley Lindberg is the editor of *The Georgia Review,* one of this country's foremost literary journals. Since its beginnings in 1947, the journal has been printed letterpress. In 1978 when the local printer in town ceased training its own Linotype operators, and the pages filled up with rivers, bad inking, and poor hyphenation, the *Review* began its long association with Heritage Printers. Lindberg talks about his reasons for staying with hot metal. In the end, it is the service and flexibility that he finds so essential:

"We are old-fashioned. I like the letterpress. We have had to go out for competitive bids but the offset people are not particularly interested in short-run work. I suspect, at some point in the future, we'll have to do our own type, but Heritage is a class operation.

"We were one of the last of the little journals to still print hot type. We were followed by *Sewanee, Virginia Quarterly,* and *Grandstreet.* I believe Heritage now does type for Atheneum—they want that human character in addition to the technology. It is curious to embrace old technology as being more human than new. I think our letterpress presents a certain character. Besides, I can't tell a computer to do what a human hand can do. Like throwing in a little extra lead.

"When I tell a computer typesetter that I'd just like a little more space here, can he reset a line, there is a lot of bitching and moaning. They don't do it, but you say to a hot-lead man, 'Can you throw more lead in there, can you reset these lines?' he'll do it.

"There are cases where I'll look at a poem and say, this poem gets destroyed by breaking it here. Can we do two long pages? Shave a little off, run it a line long? The final result is a better poem, both from a visual standpoint and a literary one.

"The reason I embrace the hot-metal technology is because of the human beings involved—it's not just the technology. With computer typesetting, they'll immediately tell you the limitations involved. But with the hot lead—this supposedly inflexible craft—they'll oblige. They take genuine pride in their work."[24]

Training: The Poor Man's College

> A Printer's case is a better education
> than a high school or a college.
> Horace Greeley

Economist and labor historian John Commons vouched for the education he received at the case: "It was in these country newspapers and job offices that my brother and I learned the printing trade, beginning at thirteen years of age, in vacations and out of school hours. This was an all-round education for us. . . ."[25]

Before the proliferation of machine work, a young apprentice would have been assigned the task of hand composition where, under the close guidance of older journeymen printers, he learned the rules of spelling, punctuation, capitalization, and typesetting. An apprentice was expected to learn by doing. When a first-year apprentice in Halper's *Foundry* is found reading a manual on electrotyping, he is reprimanded by his foreman, "Start proofing! . . . To hell with reading books, learn your trade!"[26]

In addition to gaining grammatical and technical knowledge on the job, the apprentice was indoctrinated in the social traditions and customs of the printing trade. Because of the mandated low ratio of apprentices to journeymen in printing, this social and technical system of training remained strong, with rites of passage to emphasize the change in status from apprentice to journeyman.[27]

There were occasions for printers to learn from each other outside of work as well. Earl Powell talks with enthusiasm about a group that would meet every Saturday afternoon in the 1930s, in Atlanta. "The work week was forty-eight hours then. There would be twenty-five or thirty people gather on Saturday afternoons in one of the supply houses there. There was more printing done there than there was all during the week in all the plants!"

"What would you do there?"

"Oh, we'd just talk printing."

I sigh, thinking how much I would have liked to be a fly on *that* wall.

Earl continues. "We'd talk about problems and the way to solve them. It was just a group that wanted to learn." [28]

Another invaluable resource for printers of Earl's generation was the *Inland Printer.* Cliff Gallant, who was referred to as "a literary man" by his fellow residents at the Union Printers Home, spoke highly of the *Inland Printer.* "At one time, it was the best teacher for young printers." Earl Powell agrees. "Back in the earlier days, the *Inland Printer* was a very good magazine. It showed specimen reviews and you could look at other printed pieces that were good. You could sort of study that and get a balance of design and style. In fact, to do it, you had to eat it, sleep it, drink it, and live it." [29]

Enthusiasm for the trade journal can be found in print, not surprisingly, in the pages of the *Inland Printer.* Here is a letter to the editor from a Sioux City fan:

> I wonder if you folks on the staff of THE INLAND PRINTER realize and appreciate just what your magazine means to printers—especially to boys learning the trade in small country towns. . . . Why, exactly, are so many country printers tasteful, artistic and original in the conception and design of printed forms? The answer is, here in this section of the Middle West at least—THE INLAND PRINTER. Every good printer I have ever met during my twenty years' experience in the printing industry has been a close reader and student of your excellent journal. [30]

The printer's apprenticeship served as a practical education which engendered an interest in words beyond their visualization in physical form. Those printers who aspired to be writers benefitted greatly by their education at the case, which enabled some to write articles for the newspapers on which they were working. It was not unusual in the late nineteenth century for a journeyman printer to become a successful editor.

Many renowned writers began their careers as tramp printers. Our literary heritage is full of examples. Walt Whitman spent part of his youth living the vagabond life of a tramp printer, an experience hinted at in his "Song of the Open Road."[31] Horace Greeley, founder of the *New York Herald Tribune,* spent twelve years as a tramp printer. Erskine Caldwell worked an entire summer turning the hand press and setting type at the plant of a local weekly newspaper, *The Jefferson Reporter,* in addition to writing news items, before he realized his boss was not planning on paying him for "learning newspapering."[32] Joel Chandler Harris, best known for his Uncle Remus stories, was a journeyman member of the Typographical Union. After learning the trade of country printer, he moved to Atlanta where he worked as a typesetter, and then a journalist for the *Atlanta Constitution.* Writer Lafcadio Hearn first worked as a compositor and proofreader before joining the news staff of the *Cincinnati Enquirer,* where he made his reputation for reporting local horror news. Samuel Clemens was apprenticed at age twelve to the weekly newspaper, *The Journal,* in Hannibal, Missouri, where he slept in the printing office and took his meals in the master's kitchen. Walt Whitman, Sherwood Anderson, William Dean Howells, and the Harper brothers, James and John, all served as apprentices in country printing offices.[33] Benjamin Franklin hardly needs mention. He is the personage most often cited by printers, proud of the literary lineage associated with their trade.

The amount and thoroughness of training these literary men experienced as young apprentices was enviable. As composing-room routines became more technically specialized, the apprentice's opportunity to acquire general skills decreased. "Already there are many operators who know nothing about setting type," wrote one printer who, at the turn of the century, was dismayed at the employers' practice of letting old-style compositors go in favor of younger men. He continued, ". . . in a short time our newspaper printers will be made up of young men who have never learned the case, and when through natural weakness they lose their employment, their condition . . . will be even worse than that of the old [composing] stick-handlers."[34]

Eminent journalist and political leader Thurlow Weed was so disturbed by the diminishing opportunities facing the young apprentice that he conjured up the disheartened spirit of Benjamin Franklin in his 1851 address to the New York Typographical Society. "Progress and mechanism have divested our art of much of its interest. I have never been able to look with complacency upon these innovations: and if our great exemplar, Franklin, could revisit earth, his spirit would grieve at the vandalism which has robbed 'press work' of all its intellectuality. Benjamin Franklin, though a good 'compositor,' was a good 'pressman' also, and worked as such from choice, while a journeyman. But now only one branch of our trade is taught to apprentices. A printer is now no longer connected with the 'pressroom.' The printer of the present day is a stranger to its healthful toil, its rich humors, its merry laughs, its habitual jests, and, I am constrained to remember, its too frequent revelries."[35]

At the 1899 ITU convention, president Samuel B. Donnelley voiced his opposition to the creation of specialists: "The 'all-round' printer has not been displaced by the typesetting machine, the specialist has. The man whose knowledge of the printing trade was limited to his ability as a typesetter on straight composition forms 95 percent of the unemployed printers today. The technical school for the apprentice should be the composing room, and his guardian should be the typographical union."[36]

Alabamian Barnie Weeks described the ideal apprenticeship: "You were really supposed to learn every job in that plant. That was part of the apprenticeship. Now some places, where you had weaker unions, they didn't always enforce that. But any union as large as this one [the Montgomery local], they did enforce that. You worked so long on the proof press. You worked so long tearing up the forms and disposing of the type there. You worked so long over in the ad alley. You worked so long on makeup. You went all the way 'round. Now you didn't get thoroughly competent on all of it, but you could do any of it. And only with experience did you become totally competent."[37]

But on-the-job training increasingly proved insufficient as time went on. Craft unions, anxious to maintain quality standards, instituted technical schools to supplement the training received by apprentices. In 1908 the ITU arranged a correspondence course through the Inland Printer Technical School in Chicago. A decade later, this course was replaced by the ITU's own "Lessons in Printing." By 1925 it became compulsory for all ITU apprentices to enroll in and complete the correspondence course.[38] While the union favored correspondence courses, employers turned to trade schools. Outside training was especially needed in the larger printing offices, where boys generally missed out on getting hands-on experience with all aspects of the trade.[39]

Today, more than a half century later, there is a deemphasis on serving prolonged apprenticeships. The student of commercial printing is more likely to attend a trade school than have the opportunity to pick up the tricks of the trade under the wing of an experienced journeyman printer.

Here is a glimpse into a present-day trade school, located in what once was the center of the nation's printing industry, New York City. Climbing the stairs to daylight from the Chambers Street IRT No. 1, on my way for a visit, the first thing I see is a 1950s-style sign: "LEARN-A-TRADE, THE MANHATTAN SCHOOL OF PRINTING." The school was indeed founded in the 1950s.

Two black men stand in the entrance having a smoke. "Is there an office?" I ask them.

"Yeah, one flight up."

I slip in and climb a steep, narrow flight of stairs. A secretary listens to my query and steps around to the counter. "Let me see if I can find someone to help you." She makes an in-house telephone call. "I'm going to send you to the school director."

I walk through a work area. Students are stripping in negatives, others are learning screen printing. I am shown into the office of John L. Kress, Jr. It seems as dated as the overhang sign: rippled glass door, scuffed linoleum floor, green upholstered swivel chairs. Kress is wearing half glasses and a green visor. We discuss the vocational school and its current curriculum. The latter is comprised of ten-week courses that prepare students for work in the printing industry, mostly prepress camera work and press-work. Not only has the school not offered any hot-type training for years, they closed down the "cold-type" class three years ago. Kress explains that the change in curriculum was due to the rapid changes in typesetting, claiming that they were "so fast that when the ten weeks were over, the info was already out of date." A ten-week course at this trade school is meant to prepare men and women for employment in today's printing industry, and its curriculum is continually updated to meet the demands of the industry.

The practical printers of the nineteenth and early twentieth centuries have been supplanted by a new crew of craftspeople who are trained to handle limited operations, in an increasingly specialized industry.[40] The benefits of hand composition and hot-metal training, and the prolonged guidance from journeymen, are lost on this generation's printers. Aware of this deficiency, Fil Valdez recalls, "I learned my trade under a bunch of good printers. Members of the Typographical Union. They knew that I was young and inexperienced and they kinda looked after me, you know. There was always somebody to protect me.

"They didn't condone any shoddy work, or anything. They figured, if I couldn't do the work, why, I didn't have any business having the card. And that was the proper way to look at it."[41]

Bob Culp recalls his own apprenticeship training: "I'll tell you, all the training I had from these old journeymen stood me in good stead. That helped me a great deal in the transition to cold type. Even though it wasn't wood, it wasn't metal, it wasn't coppers,[42] I could visualize the whole thing."

What, you might ask, could he visualize? Exactly what a page of photocomposed copy would require and look like, were it to be composed in hot-metal type. Developing an eye and the ability to interchange work techniques imaginatively continues to be of great importance to Bob on material, cognitive, aesthetic, and psychological grounds. In fact, it was his "eye" that furnished continuity in the transition to the new processes. "That's the reason they moved me many places. My judgment and my eye that would recognize things, whether it was new processes or old processes. I had an eye—I don't use the word loosely. In other words, I knew quality."

Bob is indebted to his teachers. "The environment that I was brought into was with old men. They might have been set in their ways, in the *way* they did it, to get to the end product. Their ways were right. Herman Tuchinsky. He was a little slower . . . but Herman, oh, he had an eye like I think I got my eyes attuned to. And I use this word and I feel so good. I have Herman's eyes now. You know what I mean?"

"Yeah."

"Oh, I so wish you could have talked with him. Such a little man. A little on the roly-poly side. He had come over to me, pulled me on the shirt and said, 'Bob . . .' " Bob's voice drops to a whisper, ". . . 'Let me show you something.' And it was something of my work coming through. And he says, 'It is right. It is right. But I have another idea.' And his other ideas were always better."

"So you need somebody?"

"Yes. Yes."[43]

Five months earlier, Bob had spoken similar words to me at work. "They put us with ones who were patient. A few great teachers. Bob Campbell, for one. They would say, 'Do it your way, then bring it to me and I'll tell you what's wrong with it.'

"You would take a proof, then mark it up. 'Try it my way,' they would say, while showing you how to save time. There were many unspoken kindnesses—whispered shortcuts, 'try this.' "

"What about how it looked?" I asked.

"Always your first consideration."

"One guy, when he retired, he gave me his tool. I couldn't work the rest of the day. It was a homemade tool—you couldn't buy it.

"I don't think they get as good training today. It's not as long."

He had glanced around the office, which was peopled with graphic designers and production coordinators. "I remember going over to a young apprentice [at Chilton] doing paste makeup and telling him, 'No, that's not right.' I would use [hot-metal] terms and he wouldn't have any idea what I was talking about. Slugs, reglets, quads."

Without expecting any answers, Bob asked, "How do you instill pride?"[44]

This attitude—that the training young people are getting today is comparatively poor, lacking in thoroughness, quality, and longevity—is echoed by other tradesmen belonging to the same generation. Peter Mathiessen's book about the baymen of the South Fork of Long Island teems with occupational narratives. The following excerpt focuses on the lost opportunity to learn fishing under the tutelage of a seasoned captain. Milt Miller was just fourteen when he started his apprenticeship on a dory crew in 1929.

"I suppose no one could have had a happier moment in their lives than to be asked to be one of the boat crew with a captain you had always admired and respected. . . . The honor soon became reality after the first day of rowin and pullin the large oars with every muscle put into use to make a good impression on the captain, the large blisters beginnin to appear in the palm of my hands, the achin, achin of every muscle, many that I didn't even know I had, that I must endure without a word."

Mathiessen reports that young Milt fished all summer, helping to lift the gillnets in the early fall mornings before going to school and hurrying back to help out again in the evenings. Milt continues:

"I don't think that boys today have the opportunity I had to work around somebody who would help him out, try to give him some knowledge; and a kid can pick up a lot of knowledge by just watching. Today the grown people chase the kid away, sayin he might get hurt. I used to work right around with these grown men, and the Lester boys and others that come up in a fishing family in Amagansett was raised the same way."[45]

Bob Culp made a similar statement which implied the importance of socialization and a shared sense of craft. He had just been offered a new job and was excited about it:

"And the guy that's there, that I *do* know, he's a good man too. Because he came up the way I came up.

"He came after me. I was working at Chilton a few years before he came. But he came up and got the same training that I got. So I know his background. And I know that I could fall back on him. Because I know what he can do."[46]

Remember that what we are hearing in these complaints is not the opinion of young apprentices in the process of initiation, but the words of elders looking back on their apprenticeships. In reminiscence, the trainee is seen through the eyes of a potential trainer. Time plays a crucial role in deadening the anguish of initiation. Memories of hardships—humility, servitude, burned skin, and aching muscles—are minimized by status earned and membership gained. One has only to think of the young intern's grueling hours, the dancer's blistered feet, or the graduate student's qualifying exams, to be reminded of the price paid for membership.

A passage from Beatrice Warde's *The Crystal Goblet* captures the peculiar socialization process that is perpetuated in the training of apprentices:

> When Aldus Manutius was in effect restyling book typography for Western Europe, his apprentices were probably treated like any other apprentices of that day from Michelangelo's down to the tinsmith's; that is, they were allowed the privilege of watching skilled men doing things "the right way," and the privilege of being cuffed if they failed to observe and imitate their betters closely enough. The paternal cuffs, and the commands to sweep the floor and bring in the beer, were (and still are) based on the principle that human beings value and respect their treasures

in proportion to what they paid for them, and that the price of skill is sweat and humility.[47]

In the case of the hot-metal journeyman printer, the price has been unreasonably high. Not only has his occupational status been devalued but the master/apprentice relationship of his youth is defunct, denying him the rewards of posterity. From the elder's or master journeyman's perspective, he has earned the right to functional posterity, that is, the chance to pass on semiformally his knowledge and skills. The latter, unfortunately, have become obsolete, so in addition to feeling devalued and displaced, he feels cheated. Perhaps when skilled laborers talk about lost opportunity and the passing of quality, what they are really saying is that young people have not gone through the appropriate socialization, that they have not "come up the way" they themselves did.

With this demise in view, we can now begin to understand how this generation of printers, troubled by occupational discontinuity, has come to traditionalize the present in patterned ways. The negative ramifications wrought by the technological change from hot to cold type fostered a need to validate collective experience and establish personal and cultural continuity.

Notes

1. Dan Burns, retired stonehand, tape-recorded interview, 13 September 1985.

2. Joe Malady, tape-recorded conversation in the lobby of the Union Printers Home, 2 February 1988.

3. The prestigious Meriden Gravure Company merged with the Stinehour Press of Lunenberg, Vermont, in the early 1980s. The joint business is now called the Meriden-Stinehour Press.

4. Beatrice Warde, *The Crystal Goblet: Sixteen Essays on Typography* (Cleveland and New York: World Publishing Company, 1956), 136.

5. Annenberg, *Typographic Journey*, 393.

6. Paul K. Wright, participant in "The Robot Revolution," *Nova* Program 1214, Public Broadcasting System, 29 October 1985, copyright 1985 WGBH Educational Foundation.

7. Cockburn, *Brothers*, 121.

8. Harley S. Shaiken, Research Associate at Massachusetts Institute of Technology, participant in "The Robot Revolution," *Nova* Program 1214, Public Broadcasting System, 29 October 1985, copyright 1985 WGBH Educational Foundation.

9. "Stripping in" is the film equivalent of the mechanical pasteup process. It tends to be more accurate, and more costly, than mechanical pasteup.

10. Karen Gaines, during tour of Packard Press, 31 October 1984.

11. Halper, *The Foundry,* 253.

12. Jim Spurlock and Frank Koncel, tape-recorded interview, 2 February 1988.

13. The early automation in the printing industry brought picture scanners and automatic hyphenation programs to computer typesetting, both of which involved highly skilled jobs previously done by photoengravers and typesetters. Carl Schlesinger, personal communication, February 1990.

14. Raymond Williams, *The Country and the City* (London: Chatto and Windus, 1973), 297–98.

15. Douglas Harper, *Working Knowledge* (Chicago: University of Chicago Press, 1987), 22.

16. Dick Harrison, interview, 24 October 1983.

17. Barbara Smith, "Allen Byrne: The Last of the Tramp Printers," *Goldenseal* 15, no. 1 (1989): 13.

18. The issue of the printer's decline in occupational status is discussed in Rogers and Friedman, *Printers Face Automation,* 6; Cockburn, *Brothers,* 31, 122–14, 129–32; and Elizabeth Faulkner Baker, *Displacement of Men by Machines: Effects of Technological Change in Commercial Printing* (1933; reprint, New York: Arno Press, 1977), passim.

19. See I. C. Cannon, "The Social Situation of the Skilled Worker: A Study of the Compositor in London," *Sociology* 1 (1967): 165–85.

20. Dan Burns, tape-recorded interview, 13 November 1985.

21. Bertram Powers, interview, 1 November 1985.

22. Dan Burns, tape-recorded interview, 13 September 1985.

23. Staff printer on the *Monterey Herald,* quoted in Marion Dearman and John Howells, "Computers Versus Craftsmen: The Case of the International Typographical Union," *California Sociologist* (Winter 1980): 55–56.

24. Stanley Lindberg, editor of *The Georgia Review,* personal communication, 30 January 1986.

25. John Commons, *Myself* (New York: Macmillan, 1934), 12.

26. Halper, *The Foundry,* 44.

27. A. J. M. Sykes, "Industrial Rite de Passage," *Man* 65 (1965): 85–86.

28. Earl Powell, tape-recorded interview, 13 November 1986.

29. Cliff Gallant, tape-recorded interview, 5 February 1988, and Earl Powell, tape-recorded interview, 13 November 1986.

30. "Why Country Printers Are Tasteful," *Inland Printer,* September 1925.

31. Hicks, *Adventures of a Tramp Printer,* 143.

32. Erskine Caldwell, *Call It Experience: The Years of Learning How to Write* (New York: Duell, Sloan and Pearce, 1951), 16.

33. W. J. Rorabaugh, *The Craft Apprentice: From Franklin to the Machine Age* (Oxford: Oxford University Press, 1986), 87, 197–99.

34. "The Wages of Compositors," in Annenberg, *Typographic Journey,* 626.

35. Address quoted in *The Life of Thurlow Weed,* vol. 2 (Boston, 1884), 192.

36. Tracy, *History of the Typographical Union,* 577.

37. Barnie Weeks, tape-recorded interview, Montgomery, Alabama, 12 December 1988.

38. Loft, *The Printing Trades;* see his discussion of union-controlled apprenticeships, 56–57.

39. For a detailed account of how the International Typographical Union handled the training of apprentices during the transition to cold composition, see Kelber and Schlesinger, *Union Printers and Controlled Automation.*

40. Loft, *The Printing Trades,* 57.

41. Fil Valdez, tape-recorded interview, 5 February 1988.

42. A copper is a thin spacing material measuring one-half point in thickness. Bob Culp, told to me during work, 24 October 1985.

43. Bob Culp, tape-recorded interview at Kelly and Cohen's, Philadelphia, 14 March 1986.

44. Bob Culp, told to me during work, 24 October 1985.

45. See Peter Mathiessen, *Men's Lives: The Surfmen and Baymen of the South Fork* (New York: Random House, 1986), 27.

46. Bob Culp, tape-recorded interview, 14 March 1986.

47. Warde, *Crystal Goblet,* 99.

7

The Rhetoric of Tradition: Occupational Narrative

The "good old times"—all times when
old are good—

Byron, *The Age of Bronze*

Dan Burns had just finished telling me of his preference for the old way of composing type in metal when he caught himself in a little self-criticism. "Talk to anybody—they all will say the old ways are better anyway. Right?" A simple answer might have come from John Peckham, longtime employee of Meriden Gravure, who was quick to point out that "everyone has a golden era." Fair enough, yet how good were the old ways when new? How does a noisy, dirty, and dangerous world come to be a source of selective reminiscence and pride? Why do we find so many people speaking nostalgically about a traditional way of life now past? Why don't printers do the opposite and vilify the old days, in order to distance themselves?

Structure: Themes, Genres, and the Folklore of Time

Printers have clearly established ways of talking about their occupational past. Nuggets of nostalgia run like a vein through their rhetoric of displacement. The rhetoric itself is an encapsulation of the printers' approach to work—an ideal established and maintained by generations of prideful printers.[1] Old-timers inform newcomers, ritualized acts are repeated, recurring activities are given names, and the relevance of tradition is given prominence through talk of an exemplary past.

Though they may not have a name for their rhetorical usage of the past, printers *are* aware of preserving their trade identity through the power of speech. Whether generalizing their experience or narrating specific incidents, journeymen printers have founded a world as tangible and nonnegotiable as the foundry type and hot-metal slugs they once handled. That hot-metal typesetting and letterpress printing are no longer viable choices for the majority of commercial and book printers only increases their symbolic value.

The printers' rhetoric of tradition is rooted in active occupational nostalgia: the old ways are better. The primary focus of such talk is the comparative decline of quality and the printers' loss of control in the work world today. Embedded within these golden-age narratives is a subtext of complaint: producing the work is now less satisfying. What is paper and paste compared to lead and wood? Our successors are mere paperhangers.

Their nostalgic plea bespeaks a reluctance to accept their technological redundance, forced upon them a generation ago. Their loss was society's gain. The fact is, typesetting has become cheaper and faster. Resolution has improved and corrections can be made more easily. Overall, the quality of *work* is arguably better. And yet, printers who once worked in metal perceive a decline in the quality of *working*—gone is the old-time independence, the craft, and the high union wages. What is lost is the life.

Themes of Talk

The printers' past is kept very much alive in spoken narrative—in conversations, in reminiscences, in definitions, in pedagogical explanations, in complaints, in stories, and in jokes. There is a thematic integrity to this narrative activity. Individual speakers typically gravitate toward one or more topics out of the following list of subjects: old-style printers, status, craftsmanship, explication of trade terms and processes, quality (both the necessity of it and the loss of it), tangibility of hot metal, pride, working conditions, accidents, initiation pranks, apprenticeships, tough bosses, memorable coworkers, being laid off, and the transition to cold-type processes. Like an assortment of foundry type, these topics lay ready to be picked out and reassembled on the composition stick of occupational narrative. It is as if, through osmosis, an unstated rule had been absorbed: These are the things a printer must talk about; these are the lessons of tradition.

Let us take one of the above themes—quality—and listen to how a number of individuals approach the topic. While reading the following four examples, keep in mind the stance taken by individual speakers, the supporting data drawn on to illustrate a point, and the overall message conveyed.

It is Tuesday, 24 October 1983. I am having lunch in the Datacomp cafeteria with Ed Jacob, Dick Harrison, and a mutual friend of ours, Mark Simos. Ed has just finished explaining the spacing advantage that Monotype has over Linotype composition. The former provides a better character fit. To make a point about quality, Ed juxtaposes examples of good and bad:

"Compare *Time* magazine to early *Time*—the hyphenation, the kerning, the legends. The best periodicals being printed today maintain the traditional optimization of typography: *National Geographic, Arizona Highways, Scientific American, Computer World.* The problem today is a degenerative one; people aren't trained.

"There has been a compromising away of quality. Even the good houses today are down to the cellar shops, the quick and dirty printing of yesterday. There is a deteriorization of readability. Reading is supposed to be a painless process.

"Take my son's textbook—a West Point calculus text. Like the service, it's loaded with deadwood. It has an eighty-page addendum! The math department had printed it to identify all the [typographical] errors in the calculus text. This is the way the world is today."

The next example comes from a 1985 interview/visit with

retired stonehand Dan Burns. I had driven out to his house in Wallingford, Pennsylvania, in the early evening. Entering his no-foyer suburban ranch house, one walks directly into the living room. Dan introduces me to his wife, who quietly retreats and remains out of sight for the rest of the evening. "I think you should sit there," Dan says, directing me to the couch, "in case you want to write anything."

He sits down in the armchair opposite the couch but gets up frequently to show me things. He has placed all sorts of instructive items on a side table, including printed matter, a composing stick, and a pica ruler. There are other things on a shelf to the side of the fireplace which he shuffles over—he is wearing slippers—to fetch. At first Dan seems worried about following an agenda, appearing smart, and "having all the right answers." Once he gets caught up in the reminiscence of occupational narrative, the formality of the interview situation subsides.

About midway through the evening Dan juxtaposes the printing quality standards he recalls from his work in hot metal with those evident in printed material today.

I ask him, "Can you elaborate on that some, give me an example?"

"Well, I'll say one thing . . ." he pauses, ". . . not only newspapers, but I mean other stuff, where they don't know how to hyphenate words."

Having made such an accusation, he recites rules memorized years ago. "Words of one syllable, or words of more than one syllable, accented on the final syllable, ending in a vowel preceded by a consonant—you double the final consonant before the . . ." he hesitates, unable to find the right word. "Like 'telling,' I see papers here, our local papers, they're carrying maybe just two letters over on the next line. It stinks.

"It stinks," he repeats. "We're not getting good reading now. You agree with me?"

"Yeah. I also agree with you about the use of rules and space. From my understanding, when you were working in metal and wood, you had to mitre things."

"We used to mitre. We used to make our own borders. Use our own heads. Make different *designs*. See? Like around Christmas, we used to make things with red berries in them. Today it's blah. I don't enjoy what I see today. During the war I worked in propaganda, four-color stuff. All these colors with perfect register. You know what I mean?"

I nod.

"With perfect alignment. Beautiful. I pick up stuff now and the red is off line."

"And do you think that's because people are in such a hurry?"

"Getting things cheaper here. That eats my heart out. There's nothing worse than some of these things you get from the Acme people; a bunch of junk. But they're probably getting it cheap. *Printing* is not cheap. You get a hold of some good magazines—see how nice things are."

"Like what would be a good magazine, a quality magazine?"

"Today?" He thinks for a minute. "Gee, we used to have *Life* . . . I don't know now . . . I could show you, I don't have one now, but I belong to the Knights of Columbus and we have a magazine called *Columbia;* the printing is beautiful. It's got a union label on it. That shows that there are craftsmen working on it. What do we have in magazines now, *Cosmopolitan?* We still have that? *Ladies Home Journal?*"

"*National Geographic* is one that people have pointed out."

"Yeah. That was mainly for good grammar and English and all. Then we have *Farm Journal, Ladies Home Companion* . . ." he giggles. "*I'm* the ladies' home companion."

The third example comes from one of my many conversations with proofreader and former Linotype operator Bob Culp. On this day, in March 1986, we are having lunch at Kelly and Cohen's, a West Philadelphia landmark. After sitting down, it is only minutes before Bob brings up the topic of quality. He believes that what has made him a valuable employee over the years is his knowledge of quality. Like Ed Jacob, he feels that inadequate training is mostly to blame for poor craftsmanship. If people work in a place that does not dictate "We want something good," after awhile, that environment will create people who will not recognize quality. Bob's juxtaposition of speed and quality is remarkably similar to Dan Burns's statement.

"Although some people might not agree with the way I do it, I think *I'm* going for quality, where *they're* going for get it out, get it out." He cites an example of several people having cut corners, which resulted in a printed piece full of poor typography. He is exasperated.

"Why can't you have quality even though the system has changed? Why should quality be sacrificed? Don't you deserve something better if it can be had? Maggie deserves better than the pulp magazine. Maggie deserves *National Geographic.*"

Later on in the conversation Bob talks about working on a top-quality magazine. "See, these were all trade magazines. They didn't go out to the general public. We had a banking magazine. *They* were very persnickety. You know the word 'persnickety'?"

I smile. He elaborates by way of example. "They wanted so much space between the paragraph and the subhead, and everything was counted. There would be so many lines in a column and if it came loose, you messed up in spacing someplace. It was a three-column magazine. They wanted all their columns straight across, line for line, even with each other. That was good work. It was a pleasure to work there."

I have heard this it-was-tough-but-we-loved-it attitude before. At the end of our lunch-hour talk, Bob recapitulates the theme; our talk ends as it began, with quality: "There are many contributing factors to a good end quality: good paper, good ink, good outlook of the person who is putting it together."

Bob's list of contributing factors is echoed in another form. The anonymous poem below was published in *The Printer,* a monthly for printers and printing history enthusiasts.

> If types be good and paper nought
> Fair printing cannot well be wrought.

If ink be good and paper ill,
The printing is imperfect still.
If all three be good, yet printers' art
And skillful hand must play their part.[2]

Continuing our conversation, Bob Culp insists: "Even with all the transition to all these new processes, there is no excuse to sacrifice quality. You probably get tired of hearing me talk about quality, but it shouldn't be sacrificed. I don't think it's a utopia."

"You don't?"

"No, no, no, no. They know they've got the speed on the new processes. So, that's one big hurdle right there. They've got the speed, the opposition has got the same thing, so why sacrifice quality? You ready to go?"

The last example is taken from a 1986 conversation between two printers, Earl Powell and Bill Loftin. What began as an informal interview in Bill's office at Heritage Printers turned into more of an animated exchange between the two of them on what they, as printers, would and would not read.

Bill admits that the majority of phototypesetting today is good, *but*, ". . . I see so many magazines . . . like my wife, we have Lutheran Brotherhood, an insurance policy that her father took out for her fifty-something years ago. And they send out a house organ, I guess would be the technical term for it. The Lutheran Brotherhood, nationwide insurance company. And I don't even want to read the magazine. Or even try to read an article because of the phototype.

"To my eye," Bill laughs, "it doesn't flow. I think the biggest problem, in the beginning certainly with phototypesetting, was the interword spacing. And they still haven't licked that in every instance."

"Nope," says Earl.

"It's a subtle thing." Bill raises himself up from his chair. "I've got an example I'll show you." He walks out of the office and over to a nearby wall of shelves filled with hardcover books. In no

It is fair to say that the vast majority of Americans have no doubts about the rightness of the colonists' break with England. The phrase "the American Revolution" causes a certain glow even in the most entrenched conservatives, who would never revolt against anybody except a new revolutionary and who, in the Revolutionary War, would most probably have been on the Loyalist side. This is because Americans are taught a very simple view of their revolution—that it was a straightforward crusade against a tyrannical Parliament and a hysterical king an ocean away. Of course, no revolution was ever so simple, certainly not this one. But patriotism, a bad historian, writes the most beguiling history, since it always offers a flattering explanation of a complicated story and satisfies our insatiable hunger for good guys and bad guys.

Fig. 44. Knopf example of typesetting.

time he returns with an oversize book written by Alistair Cooke. He opens it to a chapter opening page where a loose page of sample proof serves as a bookmark.

"This is an exaggeration, but it makes the point. This is a book published by Knopf, one of the finest names in publishing. [Alfred] Knopf died recently in the last year, ninety-something years old. But his publishing firm was known, has *always* been known, for the quality of their books. In fact, we print books for them. We have some work in here right now. They think that to uphold his whatever, charisma, that they still want to do a few books in hot metal. We're doing them.

"Anyway," Bill returns to the book in hand, "this was devastating to me because here was one of the finest names in publishing and here's one of the biggest names," Bill points to the author's name. "Couldn't put together a better package. And they set this thing in cold type.

"Well, the design, everything about it is a travesty. I couldn't believe Knopf had their name on it. But the type in this thing would be, you know, a very, very small cost. No matter what you set it in. You could set it in Monotype, the most expensive. It

It is fair to say that the vast majority of Americans have no doubts about the rightness of the colonists' break with England. The phrase "the American Revolution" causes a certain glow even in the most entrenched conservatives, who would never revolt against anybody except a new revolutionary and who, in the Revolutionary War, would most probably have been on the Loyalist side. This is because Americans are taught a very simple view of their revolution—that it was a straightforward crusade against a tyrannical Parliament and a hysterical king an ocean away. Of course, no revolution was ever so simple, certainly not this one. But patriotism, a bad historian, writes the most beguiling history, since it always offers a flattering explanation of a complicated story and satisfies our insatiable hunger for good guys and bad guys.

Fig. 45. Heritage example of typesetting.

would still be a small amount of money compared with, I don't know how many tens of thousands of copies they might have printed.[3] So the additional cost may have been out to the fourth decimal point, to have *set* the *type right.*" He taps the book with his pen for emphasis on these last few words.

"Somebody gave this to my son-in-law as a birthday present. And I was so . . ." he shakes his head as if to swear, then laughs, ". . . mad. Says, I'm gonna set that and send it to Alfred Knopf. This was before I was doing work with them.

"Well, I never did." Bill holds up the bound book and a loose page of text and explains, *"This* is hot type and this is the photo-type. The same words in the same *typeface.*"

"What typeface is that?" I ask.

"It's Garamond No. 3."

Earl eyes the Knopf page and grins. "Space wide enough to run a freight car through." I have heard this analogy appropriately updated by a younger generation. Computer typesetters working in cold type will ask each other, "Is it big enough to drive a truck through?"

Bill points to the hot-metal page he set and says, "You don't have to know what the words are. All you gotta do is look at the page and you realize that these are words on a page." Waving his hand over the faulty phototypeset page he says, "These—you know it's words, but to me it's more like alphabet soup."[4]

"Just terrible," adds Earl.

"But it's the space *between* the letters as much as the space between the words that bothers me. They just don't hang together in the words. They're words, but you don't read it like you read this," he rattles the hot-type page in front of my face.

"Now like I said, this is an exaggeration but it's the area that bothers me about photocomposition."

This time it is Earl who is complaining. "My daughters give me a lot of books. The recent books that they've given me, one in particular, I wouldn't . . . I wouldn't . . . I wouldn't even read it because of the type!" Bill lets out a short laugh before Earl continues.

"It just irritates me so bad—"

Bill overlaps him. "That's like one of these free newspapers that comes to my door. In fact, I had one there this morning—"

"Yeah, I did too."

"—the typography is so bad that I will not read it."

Indignant, Earl proclaims, "I will not either." We all begin to laugh at this point. Leaning forward in his chair, Bill says, "I pick it up and I throw it in the trash!"

The thematic consistency in these four excerpts is reinforced by congruences in attitude and rhetorical form. All of the above speakers feel a necessity to pass judgment on material examples. They praise work done in the past by enlisting a corps of exemplary magazines. They also call attention to and disassociate themselves from current-day examples of poor printing. In their discussion of the latter, Ed Jacob, Bill Loftin, and Earl Powell are motivated to explain how they possess or have come in contact with such tacky books; we are told that it is Ed's son's textbook, Bill's son-in-law's history book, and Earl's daughter's gift, or unsolicited mail, that are being criticized.

All five individuals express dissatisfaction in reading poorly set copy and carelessly printed texts. Some even refuse to do so.

Not only is reading supposed to be a "painless process," it is to be an aesthetically pleasing experience. As Moxon put it, composition should be "pleasing to the curious eye."[5] The lessons of tradition, encapsulated in narrative discourse on quality, help to ensure the prospect of such an experience.

Genres of Talk

Genre has been described as structured expectation, the "what" of recurring activity.[6] On the level of verbal discourse, this activity might include such familiar forms of speech as telling an anecdote, holding a conversation, making an announcement, repeating a rumor, placing an order, reporting the weather, making a salespitch, or conducting an interview. All are examples of the culturally recognizable ways of communicating that native speakers learn to distinguish among and manage in their daily lives. Effective social communication relies heavily on mastering such behavior, which is patterned and, to some degree, predictable.

Printers, like any other occupational group, are socialized into the complex of techniques, customs, and modes of expressive behavior that characterize their trade.[7] It is easy to discern patterned behavior in the use of trade jargon, the restaging of initiation pranks, and the justifying of a line of type. But what about the overall narrative environment in which printers talk about their occupation and their occupational past? Is there a rhyme to the reason?

We have already noted the consistency in *what* talk is about. Within these themes, printers choose from a repertoire of expressive forms. Sometimes the genre of speech is framed by the speaker, as in Bert Powers's reference to "stories" (i.e., lies):

We had got onto the topic of work shifts. I ask what the name for the late-night shift was.

"The lobster shift."

"Why lobster?"

"Oh, there's lots of *stories*. Some say it's 'cause you worked from 11:00 P.M. to 8:00 A.M. and could go to the beach, lie in the sun, and turn red. It ain't true. I worked on the lobster shift once. We'd get off at 7:00 or 9:00 [in the morning] and go back to an apartment with no heat. The landlords would turn it off at 10:00, so you went and had a drink.

"Course that wasn't the only reason." [8]

Many stories circulate about the etymology of "lobster shift" for the late-night work shift. In the late 1800s most newspapers in New York City were on Printers' Row (also called Newspaper Row and Park Row), which was just a few blocks from the Fulton Fish Market. If printers took their lunch at 4:00 or 5:00 A.M., it was possible to walk to the fish market and eat fresh lobster, as it was coming off the boats at that hour. [9]

Legendary figures in the printing world and their peculiar habits are the sources of tales that circulate in oral and written tradition. Horace Greeley was notorious not only for his editorial skills but for his illegible handwriting. The following story, which falls into the category of pranks and is well-known among printers, was relayed to me by Archie Green.

"In 1941, I met a fine printer and active ITU member, Paul Aller, at the Grabhorn Press in San Francisco. To illustrate a compositor's skill, Paul told me this story:

"Horace Greeley had terrible handwriting—the world's worst. Only one compositor on the *Tribune* could read the editor's scrawl. This old hand did not let anyone else set the daily editorials. One day, the other printers became tired of the old hand's constant boasting. They went out, found a young chicken, and brought it back to the composing room. The men dipped the chicken's claws into the ink pot. Then, they let the chicken walk all over a page of Greeley's foolscap [paper size 13½ by 17 inches]. They gave this marked foolscap to the old compositor. It did not phase him. He just stood proudly at his case, read the chicken claw marks, and set the type for a thundering editorial on slavery. Greeley never let on that he smelled a joke. But the printers ragged the old hand about his reading skill. Finally, the laughter got to the old hand, and he quit." [10]

Every printer I spoke with had stories about the pranks that were played on greenhorns. Most recounted the experience as victims, a few as accomplices. All called them pranks. But what of the unnamed categories of communication which characterize printers' talk? Though the printers have no explicit name for what they engage in, language use reveals three ways of speaking: explication, statements of identity, and storying.

The genre of explicating trade terminology and work processes differs stylistically from statements of identity and membership. The former is pedagogic in nature and involves step-by-step description, often accompanied by picture drawing and inquisitive monitoring at regular intervals, e.g., "'Kay?" "Okay?" "You get the feel of what I'm saying?" These metacommunicative[11] queries by the speaker underscore the importance of what has just been said.

For example, note how Dick Harrison punctuates his speech with these queries as he explains the phrase "the type is off its feet." The salient points are italicized for emphasis.

"*Okay,* now a piece of type, foundry type, when it was cast it had a flash removed that gave the base of the letter two very smooth surfaces, and then a groove in the middle, and it looked like two feet. *Okay?*

"Now what would happen when you assemble the letters in a stick and you'd get them in crooked, the letters would be canted somewhat. And then when it would print you'd get a real hard edge on one part of the *H* and the other part would disappear. So the type was 'off its feet.' *'Kay?*"

A few minutes after explaining this, Dick shows me a composing stick. "There's some teeth on the side here, on the bottom, *see?* And teeth in here. And here's a half-pica lever; you could go halfway. You'd swing this over to the other side and it would be very accurate parallel sides. So when you pushed the type off its feet, it would stand without flopping down. That's the justification. That's the feel you get." [12]

Note the similarity in form between the remarks above and

Ed Jacob's explication of the term "turtle" below. Both accounts alternate between description of technique, possible blunders involved in performing such technique, and metacommunicative checks on the description itself.

"Hot metal. You have these big stones where you make up the pages. Now stone isn't the proper word. These were steel. Stone would wear out. But they still call it a stone, *okay?*

"And, 'course there were galleys in here. These were quite large. Maybe four by six feet. Had a little lip here, if you looked at it sideways it was like this." *He draws a side perspective of the stone.*

"*Okay,* now this is where all your type would stand in the frame and all. Now, when you want to move that, especially in a newspaper shop, they bring a turtle over. It's nothing but another one [stone] with wheels on it. And there's a little lip in there and you can just slide it on over. Because many times, in a newspaper, you can't lock it up in the chase tight enough to lift it. Book shop, you must. But in a newspaper, you slide. It's not made up that well, there's not enough time, *okay?*

"You know the principle of the chase? You have all your type. Then you have your wedges. *Right?*" *Ed has drawn a rectangular box and points to the four corners of the chase with the tip of his pen: "Here, here, here, here."*

I ask where the key goes in and he shows me with the pen. "Right here, the key fits in like this. It forces these wedges so it presses down on here, and locks this in. Locks it against that edge. Now, other than in newspaper, that has to be tight enough to lift without anything falling out. And I'll tell you, if something falls out, the whole goddamn thing falls out. *Right?* It does.

"So, newspapers can't do that. They don't have the time. They can't risk losing the page. They had turtles all over the place."[13]

While this talk is informal and participatory, other talk is less a dialogue about process and more a monologue about identity. Such statements are often delivered as simple truths, epigrams which do not invite question. Here the rhetoric of tradition is expressed most clearly. Spoken with a sense of evaluative reflex-

ivity, these statements have a way of drawing attention to themselves; they are short, conclusive, emphatic, and often contain repetition of key phrases. Sometimes the identity statement is prefaced with an explicit reference to tradition. Ed continues:

"If you had a nice customer, the proofreader could edit the
page. Mark the manuscript, 'edit, page fit' or something like that.
The customer knew he did that to make a good page break. If he
didn't, the proof comes back and they would mark, 'take that
word out, reset these lines, but pick this up.' Now that was a
common understanding in book work. It was a courtesy of *tradition*
between good typesetters and good publishers.

"It was important to build up that respect for each other.
They had the confidence that you wouldn't put in some stupid
word, or you wouldn't take the principle phrase out, *okay?*

"*Proofreaders were proofreaders then, born copycats.* 'Kay? It made
the difference. And invariably, the customer also had proofreaders
backing up the editors. Not today, not today. Even printers don't
have good proofreaders." [14]

Notice that the identity statement about proofreaders is
couched between two monitoring queries.

What at first seems to be a tautologically insignificant definition turns out to be a familiar form of speech among printers.
The noun in question is simply repeated, as in, "A _____ was
a _____, back then." A similar dynamic is at work in phrases such
as "He is a musician's musician," "La crème de la crème," or "Anybody who's anybody would. . . ." Below are examples of this kind
of statement embedded in conversation. This exchange took place
in Bill Loftin's office at Heritage Printers.

I had just expressed some confusion over the term "printer"
as it applied to the individual employees at Heritage. Though I
inquire about current-day practice, both Bill Loftin and Earl Powell answer in the past tense.

"Tradition." Bill says, "The printer was the compositor in
tradition."

"That's right," attests Earl.

Bill continues. "He was a typographer, he was a—"

Earl completes the sentence. "He was a printer."

We have come full circle, as if the terms "printer," "compositor," and "typographer" are either synonymous or self-evident. They continue to alternate, taking turns with definitive statements.

"He was a man of wisdom, so to speak, in the operation," Bill adds and gives a small laugh.

"*A Linotype operator is a Linotype operator,* the man that ran the press was the pressman," states Earl.

Bill adds, "You had the floorman. But the printer was sort of the super of the composing room."

"That's right. He was the one who put it together and chose the display types and—"

"Artwork," says Bill. "The copy, what to set it in. And actually made the form up. The printer, that was the printer."

"Which you've both done?" I ask, looking at each of them in succession.

Bill concedes, "Well, Earl is the printer. Earl is the real *trueblood printer.*" [15]

Others associate printer identity with unionism. When Amelia Story speaks of her boss, she invokes the brotherhood ideally shared by all union printers. "My boss was a *true printer.* And a brother printer. You know, they belonged to the union. And they believed in brotherhood." [16]

The majority of identity statements are composed in the past tense and they tend to refer to a generalized time or era, rather than a specific individual or incident. Once the speaker shifts his focus from the general to the particular, the identity statement may serve as a narrative element in a story. For example, Earl Powell made the following identity statement concerning the definition of a printer: "Well, a true printer is a person who takes pride in setting type that's pleasing to the eye." Minutes later, after letting Bill take his turn at describing what printing is like "nowadays," Earl speaks up, only this time his definition takes the form of a story:

"Never will forget, many years ago, back during the Depression years, at the plant that I worked in Atlanta, the estimating department estimated the time it would take to do a job, and if you went over that, you did that for nothing. You didn't get paid for it.

"And we had a job that was a reprint job that was horrible and the same plant had done it before. And when I redid it, I kerned the capital letters. I tried to do it right.

"Well, I went over about thirty hours; it was a big job." Bill whistles. Earl continues. "And the superintendent called me up there, Mr. Deke Zatco was his name, and he told me how much I'd gone over. He said, 'Now why, why did it take you that much longer?'

"I said, 'Well, I put that much more into it.'

Bill, an employer himself, laughs at Earl's answer. "It was a two-color job. It had to be broke for color. I said, 'Well, wait till the customer gets it and wait till it goes through the pressroom. And we'll decide whether I put more into it or not.'

"When the job was bound and delivered, well, he come back to me and bring me my extra pay and ten dollars plus."

More laughter from Bill, the moral to the story clear. "Well, that's the best example of the difference with the present," he says.

"And ten dollars was ten dollars then," Earl adds.[17]

When printers get around to discussing the more intangible qualities of a good printer, they will often talk about "having an eye." Note how John Peckham moves from a general statement about quality in craftsmanship, to a discussion about a group of workers, to a story about a specific individual, ending up with a general statement about the craftsman's eye.

"It's the quality of the man that makes the difference. You have to have an eye." He follows this emphatic statement with a technical discussion of collotype printing, explaining that the inking is done by hand with a putty knife.

"The ink wouldn't get to the plate until twenty-five impressions. Pressmen had to be sensitive. Some people—very intelligent kids—you could take two prints, side by side, and they couldn't tell the difference. Color blindness. There is such a thing as image incapacity.

"These pressmen were absolutely fantastic. There was variation. You were hand inking. Irv Breckman was a pressman, a barrel-chested guy. When he left he had more than fifty years here."

Then, in what seems like a non-sequitur aside, Peckham explains that he belongs to the local rod and gun club and that the club had asked if he could print the menu for the annual dinner. "They wanted a WPA job. The picture was the worst calendar art and Irv printed it beautifully. He could *see* it. An ability to see is not necessarily a factor of taste. A lot of craftsmen have done terrible things beautifully." [18]

When I had asked Carl Gross how one learns the appropriate use of typefaces, he responded, "Through time. It takes time. And by seeing good work." [19] After Ed Jacob had spoken at great length about dressing the type, I asked him how someone would learn that kind of thing. He paused for awhile before answering. "Your eyes . . . you might even put a copper in here, if that had serifs, . . ." and he was off again, describing the process of dressing the type. [20] Bob Culp also gravitated toward the topic again and again, as mentioned above, when he said, "I had an eye—I don't use the word loosely." He added a metacommunicative message, to ensure my understanding of the phrase. "In other words, I knew quality."

"I think that was one reason I was of value." It was here that he spoke of inheriting his master teacher's eyes, ". . . but Herman, oh, he had an eye like I think I got my eyes attuned to. And I use this word and I feel so good—I have Herman's eyes now. You know what I mean?" [21]

Compositor Rick Newell still works in the hot-metal tradition. To watch him making up a sample page at a Vandercook proof press is to watch the printer's eye in action. He tightens up the form and moves his right hand to make an adjustment above the cylinder. It is a large movement requiring a good bit of energy.

After one revolution he checks his results by measuring the head margins and side margins with his pica ruler.

"I'm only three nine, that's pretty close . . . can't live with that. Yeah, I'm off a little bit." Rich compares the head margins on the verso and recto. "This side has to come up. . . ."

Rick pulls one more run through the press. "Looks good." He measures the margins, "It's still off. Went by that way a little too much."

More adjustments. Another proof. "All looks fine to me."

"What is this typeface?" I ask.

"Monticello. I *like* it. Easy to read. Prints good."

Now that Rick has gotten the form in position on the page, he makes plenty of copies. Then he moves on to print the back up, explaining the layout of sample pages. "You have your opening page here. The specs should be on the back. So if they have extracts, subheads, footnotes, we try to get a little of everything. This one here is just straight text."

Rick takes the proofs he has just printed and uses the back side to print the new material in the press. He runs the first sheet through, then holds it up to the light to check to see if the lines back up each other—what is called the "register" in the trade.

"Pretty close . . . maybe I'll tighten it just a little bit. For the first time, that's not bad," he tells me, as much as himself. A small adjustment made, he pulls another proof. He seems satisfied with it and says, while holding the page up to the light, "That's the sign of a good printer."

"What is?"

"When your lines back up." [22]

It is only after Rick has satisfactorily finished the job at hand that he stands back and makes an evaluative statement about printer identity.

In effect, printers are making statements of identity whenever they talk or tell stories about the old-style printer, the changing status of the printer, and the qualifications for membership as a printer, including those who were great and those who were not.

Even in recounting their own personal work histories printers are communicating something about the continuity of occupational identity.

The Folklore of Time

One of the most distinctive features of the printer's occupational discourse is the way in which narrated experience is temporally framed. By this I mean not only the amount of time spent talking about the past, but the consistency in how past and present are delineated and juxtaposed in the narrators' worldview. In the printer's folklore of time, a legendary past of the old-time printer antecedes the more recent past of the transition to cold type, which precedes the "nowadays" of the present. It is a conceptual, if not utilitarian, time frame, as we shall see.

Legendary Talk: "Then"

A significant portion of the printer's narrative repertoire is made up of statements and stories that tell of an earlier, pre-electronic world of printing which is now regretfully gone. These narratives recall a prior time when printers allegedly enjoyed a coveted occupational status, respect, pride, and control. Dick Harrison's complaint is representative of the genre; in his idealization of times past, he concedes, "So there's no legend, there's no aura of being a printer anymore. Like Ben Franklin said, 'Ben Franklin, *printer.*' In those days, that was something." [23]

Even as early as 1890, craftsmen were lamenting the decline of the printer's status. In the flurry of new inventions, the book printer suffered in caste and in pay. The turn-of-the-century printer's situation, one in which he was unseated by labor-saving machinery, generated a rhetoric of displacement very similar to that of our mid-twentieth-century printer. The following was penned in 1890, but it could just as easily be expressed a hundred years hence.

"Gutenberg would have been amazed could he have foreseen the consequences of evolution in the printing business. In his day, printing was little, but the printer was great. In ours, printing is the mainspring of our civilization . . . while the printer is—well, he is relegated to the domain of a common wage worker, and that would be enough to horrify the father of typography."[24]

Ed Jacob spoke about craftsmanship being common in the past. "It was the tradition then," were his words, implying a break in the continuity of craft tradition. The "then" Ed Jacob was referring to in this instance was specified, "about 1904, 1906." Then again, I had asked. He had been speaking enthusiastically about the type gems to be found in old magazine advertisements. "From what period was this?" I wanted to know, and was told. More often, however, the "then" framed in a printer's narrative is left undated and unlocalized: "When I was young, even before my time, printers used to wear high hats; they were supposed to be artists," "In the past, a printer was a specialist," "In the older days, . . ." The flexibility of this nominal "then" is like that of a movable "do" in music;[25] the "now" of one person's life will surely serve as the "back then" of another's.

A person's relation to the past is relative to that person's place in it. It is like the literary nostalgia for the earlier country life of Old England described by Raymond Williams in *The Country and the City*. When Williams moved back in time in search of that earlier, happier England, he could find no place or period in which to rest seriously.[26] This search is our "movable then," which denotes life not as it really was but as it is conceived to have been. One *Inland Printer* 1925 editorial pokes fun at this nostalgic impulse in a piece entitled "The Good Old Days that Never Were."

The good old days evoked in the printer's rhetoric of displacement are not entirely good. Though portrayed as a time of higher status, pride, satisfaction, and fellowship, it is not a pollyanna past. The majority of printers speak of an odious environment and tough working conditions—the heat, the chemicals, the accidents, and the long hours they experienced. After Earl Powell's story about overtime at an Atlanta plant, Bill Loftin said, "Well, tell her about how you'd go to work on Monday sometimes and not come home until Saturday."

"Well, I've worked many a time all day, all night and all day, and well into the next night!"

"Really?!"

"Lots of times."

"That's one difference today," Bill says.

Enjoying the reminiscing, Earl continues. "We had one job that had to be handset. It was a ladies shoe catalog. It had to be handset once a month. We had to run the type around those long high heels . . ."

Bill and I laugh. ". . . and another printer and me, well, we'd work all day all night and all day the next day and usually we'd get through about six or seven o'clock the next night."

"Geez," I shake my head. Bill laughs with incredulity and asks, "How many typographical errors did you have in *those* proofs?"

"Well, we really didn't do too bad on it."

"Golly Pete, twenty-four, thirty-six hours. You must have been ready to . . ."

"Did you eat there?" I ask.

"Yeah, we'd just get a sandwich and keep going."

Bill remembers something. "I thought you were telling me that during yearbook season, people would *sleep* on the floor."

"Well, I have seen that done in the last part of it. I know we'd start off in early March or late February working from 7:30 in the morning to 9:42 at night. That was back when we's working forty-eight hours a week. During the regular workweek we worked from 7:30 in the morning to 4:42 in the afternoon with thirty minutes for lunch.

"Was this union?" I ask.

"No, this wasn't then, no. Then as the season got a little older we printed about 120 to 130 different yearbooks. Big ones at that. So then they'd step it up to 10:42, 11:42 . . . ," his voice increasing in speed and volume, ". . . 12:42, 1:42, 2:42!"

A "my God," from Bill.

"Along near the end, if they didn't deliver on time, they'd have to mail them out and boy, that would run into money."

"As soon as they got the last one out, you didn't get to work at all, wasn't that it?" Bill asks.

"Well, they lay you off at twelve o'clock if you didn't have anything to do. They'd either lay you off at twelve o'clock or three o'clock. So you had to make that money in order to make a living.

"Thank goodness those days are gone. It's still a fascinating business though."[27]

The subtext to this and other stories about tough times reads: thank goodness we do not have to work like that today, but at least we were capable of it. Meeting those challenges made us what we were. The nasty details of the unremitting dirt, the unattainable standards, and the unbearable noise and heat are included as living proof that "people were tougher then." It may have been bad, but they were good old bad old days.

The wonder of a romanticized past lies in its nonnegotiability. Conditions are created for a certain kind of exchange that permits people to talk about things otherwise unspeakable. Telling a story out of the past, to one who was not there, is an achievement of social distancing.[28] This is true whether one is talking about the distant past of the old-style printer or whether one is speaking about the transitional times of the more recent past.

Changing Talk: "What Happened"

Like any memorable event or dramatic occurrence, the change to cold type during the 1950s through the 1970s generated a new kind of narrative. The experiential world of the traditional printer had been shaken by the introduction of new technology. Unlike any previous technological innovations, this one promised to threaten the very existence of the compositor. In the retrospective narrative world of the hot-type printer, the disruption needs explaining.

Rather than the status-quo description of an old-world environment, talk shifts to active description befitting a time of transition. Having been oriented to the world of "what was," we enter the realm of "what happened." The demise of hot metal is recounted. The sudden though temporary drop in typographic quality is explained. Blame is laid on the art and advertising world for taking over the traditional domain of the printer. Either the "old-timers were retiring in droves," as John Peckham put it, or they accommodated the change, as Bob Culp judged: "He was an old-time printer but in the end, he was just putting time in running the machines." The time of transition is described as a no-win situation, especially for those who were unprepared for the change, refusing to believe that the new processes were coming. Eighty-one-year-old Dan Burns recalls his own reluctance to believe:

"See, a lot of people resented that. In other words, we can see the end of a . . . a . . . a printing business, you know? It's gradually dying out, when that happens, see? These things are a pain in the neck," he says, gesturing to his hearing aid.

"See, technology was taking over. In fact five years before that ever happened, I was told that that was *going* to happen. But I never believed they could do what they did. And they did it."

Even if one did believe, there were other obstacles. Training programs were offered by employers as an alternative to retirement, but for some in their early sixties, like Dan Burns, the option was less than inviting.

"Today, you see, before they changed over, when they were talking about changing over, our union and other places gave the members of the union a chance to go to school and learn paste makeup. Learn how to do these things when they came in."

"The new things?"

"Yeah. I didn't go because I jumped over that." He grins. "Because, that's when they asked me to go to the front office. You either had to train in that or else. Because what are you going to do? That's all there was left to do. Bob Culp had to do it. *I* didn't do it, because I . . . ," he hesitates, "I was working on the imposition." Dan was offered a white-collar position that involved the planning of imposition layouts for the offset presses.

Later on in our conversation I asked Dan about the union's role in the technological change to cold-metal composition and he returned to the topic of retraining.

"See, that worked out all right. And the employers agreed to it and kept people on as long as they were learning what they were learning. Bob Culp was one of them. I could have done it too. I tell you, at my age, I'm not going to go to school." [29]

In contrast to narratives about disbelief, job transfers, and resignation, there are those of personal salvation. Both Ed Jacob and Bob Culp have stories about how they were spared. Ed talks about being part of a dying breed, having seen a craft disappear in his lifetime:

"The only thing that saved me was, I guess I convinced myself it was happening. And got out. And got into computerized.

"Yeah, in '68 I walked out of a place and went over to Rocappi. And fortunately, it was lucky because they wanted typesetters. They didn't want these wild young Turks who knew everything *except* typesetting. There was an extremely good programmer over there. Yeah, Scot Walden, he was a typesetter. God, what a combination. He could understand what I would want." [30]

In other words, Walden knew type, as any printer should. Ed's mention of the man's understanding is a rhetorical use of tradition just as Bob Culp's ". . . I knew the styles. I knew what they wanted" is in the following example.

Bob read the passage I lent him from John Updike's novel *Rabbit Redux,* in which Rabbit is being fired due to the changeover to offset. Bob acknowledged the disbelief of other coworkers to accept the change, before recounting his own prescience:

"[Rabbit] was the son of a guy that they evidently kept on when they were going to offset. He must have known of the new processes coming in but he kept pushing them back, you know, 'It's not going to happen to me. It's not going to happen to me.'

"Well, I *knew* that it was going to happen and I felt, well, I'm going to have to make the change with it. I had the *opportunity* to make the change with it because of the priority I had.

"It was back in the late sixties. I was one of the last in the hot metal. Then I went into the camera department. Then I started to acclimate myself to it. I heard that Kodak had courses for those in the industry. I went to Kodak, I went to other schools in the city, learning every possible angle I could. See, now here's where my basic printing . . . ," he interrupts himself, remembering another position, ". . . the pasteup department, I worked in there. Because they knew I could put a page together! And I'm using a piece of paper now. And I knew the styles. I knew what they wanted. And they knew the quality was there."

Listening to this chronology, I wanted to know more about how Bob made the switch from composing type to camera work. "When you left the hot metal, you went directly to the camera department?"

He nods, "Didn't know anything about it."

"But who was inputting the type?"

"They had a type system similar to the Varityper."

"So you didn't go from hot-metal type to keyboarding, you went to some other—"

"No."

"—kind of work?"

"That's right."

"Why was that? Just your choice or their choice?"

"I had a choice of either going into stripping or camera. I don't know why I chose that."

"But you didn't have a choice of going into . . ."

"No, I didn't have that choice." A controversial issue, "that choice" is left unspoken, though we both know it was the choice of keyboarding on photocomposition equipment. "I don't think I wanted it either," he adds.

"Why?"

"Because you're in one place too long. I like to move around. They could use me in many places."

"Did anybody go directly from a Linotype to keyboarding on—"

"Yes."

"Do you know how they felt about that?"

"They felt good. They knew they had to learn a typewriter though, 'cause the Linotype keyboard is a different keyboard. The transition was comfortable for them. They had to learn codes and so forth."

"So in some senses, this transition wasn't so bad?"

"The transition, speaking of the composing room as a whole, quantity was sacrificed. It took things a little longer until the people got acclimated into the new niche. Then quantity started to pick up. There was a quality that was lost also, because it was a new feeling. A new pair of shoes to wear. Once they got broken into it, the quality came back."

I am taken aback by this seeming contradiction, having heard Bob's refrain on the loss of quality. "It did come back?"

"Oh yes. And it wasn't long, that transition. It was surprising. It came quick. By quick I don't mean weeks, but a few months."

"So really, it's not that tragic," I suggest.

"Oh yes. There was tragedy. Now, this is the tragic part. The old-timers who didn't know how to change. Some of them really—it was like getting hit with a door. Like they closed the door on them." He imagines their anguish, "'I can't do that,' and a response, 'You can try.' Maybe they couldn't do it. Maybe they couldn't go for more schooling.

"Let's face it, some of them were in their late fifties, sixties, seventies. We had one old man who was in his nineties. There were a lot of young people there, too. I kinda think that the way it worked out, the company was glad. 'Cause some of the old-timers that tried to make the change—it was hard. Mistakes and so forth. And they were fighting it, I thought. That's a personal view, but I thought they were fighting it.

"Some were bitter. Even though they were making the change, they were bitter about it. '*Why* did you take that away? That's been good for me.'"[31]

Bob's empathy reminded me of a passing conversation I had with a Union Printers Home resident. He had stopped to pick up his mail, which is dispensed in the corner of the home's library. I had in my hand a scrapbook which was papered with illustration pages clipped from old issues of the *Inland Printer*. Charles Miner, born in 1915, took note of the illustration I was admiring. "That's the old handset. I worked on a Linotype for twenty-seven years," he tells me. "Haven't touched one since 1971. Got out of it then. When the new machines came."

"Have you seen them, the new machines?" I ask him.

"I've no interest in seeing them; they took my trade away from me." Embittered, he adds, "Used to be 100,000 members. Now there's 40,000. Back in '68, there were 400 residents here. Now there's 140."[32]

Adaptation Talk: The Comparative Present
of "Then/Now"

Probably the most ubiquitous form of talk is the printer's temporal juxtaposition of then to now. The past of the old-time printer serves as context for talk about the relative now. Rhetorical comparisons of "back then" to "nowadays" generally favor the past over the present, suggesting that this style of nostalgia is a narrative adaptation to the harsher realities of change. Whereas changing talk is explanatory in nature, adaptation talk is evaluative, a subjective commentary on the explanation of change.

We have to consider what these comparisons are about before we think about why they might be useful to those who make them. To begin with, there is the printer's language. In the beginning of this book we examined the trade-specific importance of terminology: trade jargon, how to use it properly, pranks designed around the teaching of printing terms. The language that hot-type printers shared is captured in Earl Powell's reminiscence of the Saturday gatherings where printers would "talk printing," a language between printers that "only printers would be interested in." Ed Jacob's assumption, "Everybody knew what '30 slug' meant," and Bob Culp's comment, "It was like a language. I could say nonpareil, mutt—that meant something," also attest to the uniqueness of the printer's language. It is a language as threatened as the parts and processes it was invented to describe. Recall Bob Culp's discussion of his teachers:

"They put us with ones who were patient. A few great teachers . . . I don't think they get as good training today. It's not as long.

"I remember going over to a young apprentice [at Chilton] doing paste makeup and telling him, 'No, that's not right.' I'd use terms and he wouldn't have any idea what I was talking about . . . 'slugs,' 'reglets,' 'quads.'" Bob's statement implies that the outlook for the upcoming generation is degenerating.

Carl Gross made a similar then/now statement about training:

"At RIT [Rochester Institute of Technology] we had an entire course in Linotype and Monotype. It was required. You know about required courses. Who wants to take them? That was back in 1969! And I've *never* been more excited by type than I am now. Perhaps it's my personality but I learn best by experience, by standing in front of a bank, picking click, and pieing type—now *that's* experience.

"Nowadays, students may spend one day at a Linotype machine, or simply read about the process of hot-metal composition in a book."[33]

Comparisons are made indicating that work in the trade was better in the past; recall, for example, Dick Harrison's statement: "In the past, the printer was a specialist. You abdicated all responsibility to him to do it right.

"Nowadays, it's all different. A carpenter? Today he's nothing but a hatchet man. A stonemason? He's nothing but a cinderblock man."

Or Fil Valdez's summation: "It was a romantic trade. You did things with your hands. It was creative; you did what you wanted to do.

"Now, it's not like that any more, you know. Everything is cut and dried on the machine."[34] The implication is that current-day printers experience a loss of control and a lack of satisfaction in their work.

Bertram Powers's then/now description of the hot-metal world focused on the loss of brotherhood between workers. "You were working with your hands. And you worked with each other.

Brothers—you had to work together. The Linotype handed hard copy to the handman. You had something to do with the entire project.

"Not so now."

Less comaraderie and less work. The sentiment is captured in a then/now narrative spoken by a veteran of the composing room at the *New York Times:*

"At 8:15 in the evening in the old days, you used to see two hundred guys rushing to get out the first edition. No more. One night I looked around the composing room at 8:15 and saw seven guys at terminals—all doing advance work. The edition was in already!"[35]

Even if the printer acknowledges that some things have improved (better ventilation, quieter, cleaner working environs) he more than likely will counter the improvements by expressing their negative ramifications. Printers quoted in Cynthia Cockburn's study welcome the clean, less physically demanding environment:

> "Oh it's very good, very nice. Well decorated, air conditioned. . . . It's nice to be able to come in to work with a suit on. Not to be going home each shift filthy dirty, smelling of ink. There are more seats. In hot metal you always used to stand by the case or the stone. Varicose veins were common among the older men. Whenever we go back there, now, any of us, we see the noise and the dirtiness and, everyone says, yuck! how did we stand it? The secret is, you wanted to do that work so you were prepared to accept the noise and the heat as one of the conditions. But we wouldn't want to go back."

But such appreciation is conditional; the new clean environment is no compensation for the old hot-metal atmosphere evoked in their occupational nostalgia.

> "It's not the same without that mixture of smells, the ink, the grease, paraffin. It was like a dose of everything that was good for you, you know. What does a little dirt matter after all? People

have to work and get their hands dirty, you get more satisfaction out of it than those people that sit there, you know, like a tailor's dummy at an office desk."[36]

The physically demanding and exacting work conditions described by printers, such as those mentioned in Earl Powell's story about overtime, are extended into then/now narratives. Belittling the comparatively cushy conditions of the present reinforces the legendary prowess of the old-time printers. Listen to the way John Peckham describes the conditions at Meriden Gravure before and after air conditioning:

"With collotype, we had to run the humidity. The temperature was 105 degrees. Guys stripped to the waist with towels around their necks.

"Today, when the air conditioning goes, people can't work. They get sick!"[37]

This type of comparison, which contrasts hearty, virile, old-timers to delicate, dare I say, effeminate newcomers, is corroborated in the fictional portrayal of life in a Chicago electrotype foundry. It is as if the printing trade itself has been emasculated. "In the old days we wiped our backsides with sandpaper, now the men must have silk tissue to rub against their skins. Progress!"[38]

Such examples from oral and written sources, which emphasize the endurance of workers in the past while disparaging the irresoluteness of the present generation of workers, may help restore some of the old-time printers' sense of lost esteem and power.

After all, there is plenty of talk circulating about how great printers were "back then" and less talk about how great the young printers are today. With the exception of Bill Loftin, who assured me that there are young craftsmen working in the new technology, no one sang the praises of the younger generation of printers, or spoke enthusiastically about their future. Perhaps this is compensation for the fact that printing is no longer at the center of the universe as it was once considered to be.

Ed Jacob remembers the trade in this era. "Printing was a pretty good craft for many years. And it was very large, too. It

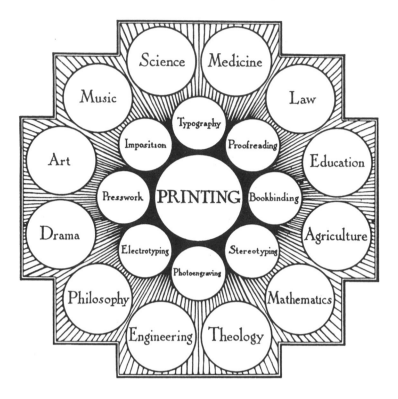

Fig. 46. Illustration from *ITU Lessons in Printing,* 1942.

was a big employer in the United States. You go back into your old statistics, the number of people employed in the printing field, in the industry, total: press, bindery everything, paper—lots of people.

"Yeah, you had so many newspapers then. So many publishers. So, technology has really reduced it tremendously."[39]

Even though Bill Loftin's hot-metal production plant is doing well, he has no plans for passing on the business, confident that there is no future in hot metal. When I ask him why he had chosen to stick with hot-metal production he chuckles and responds:

"Well, that's a good question. I guess, in one sense, for the sake of the people working here. I don't say they couldn't learn the phototypesetting, but I know that at Washburn and some other places they tried and it didn't work too well. Linotype operators really didn't make good phototypesetting keyboarders.

"It's partly that and, as I quoted Bruce Rogers, letterpress printing is virile and offset sterile. The look doesn't appeal to me. I like what we end up with. And I have this back-of-my-head feeling that, well, it may not be a big market, but it's almost no supply. At least it's a living. And these people," he gestures toward his employees, "are going to have a living. That's my goal right now. To live till the last man retires. There will be no future generation."[40]

Bill Loftin's words ring true in another part of the country. New York's once formidable craft union, Big 6, has shrunk to barely a thousand members from eleven thousand-odd members in the early 1970s. Bertram Powers, the chief architect of the "automation pact" that allowed printers' jobs to be phased out by automation, commented recently that the union was "dying by inches, if not by yards." Powers, who in the early 1960s led his union in the 114-day strike that resulted in the eventual closing of five major dailies, is acutely aware of the loss of bargaining power experienced by the printing craft unions. "Once upon a time, you struck, and you won or you lost," Powers said. "Nowadays, we Americans still have the right to strike. But if we lose the strike, we lose our jobs."[41]

The hot-type printer, unable to pass along his tools or his techniques, is somewhat reluctant about passing along his title. I ask Earl Powell about the present-day situation. "Today, anybody working with reproducing text, would you consider anybody a printer? In your mind, what would define a printer, in the sense that you think of yourself as a printer?"

"Well, I guess we'd have to define 'em as . . . ," he pauses and then lowers his voice, acknowledging a problem. "That's a good question."

"After all, they do *print,* so I guess we just still have to refer to them as printers. 'Cause to me printing is the most important business that the world's ever known. . . . Back in the older days, it was a dirty business. The working conditions were bad. I know the first day that I went to work, I was the inkiest boy that ever went home!"[42]

Function

Whether a printer was displaced in early retirement or reclassified as a stripper, camera man, or computer typesetter, he still had to come to grips with the change. An identity he had spent years preparing for, and more years embodying, had now come to an end. It is one thing to learn the new processes of automated type-setting in return for job security and voluntary retirement, but quite another to let go a craft identity. In just two decades, the craft of setting type has been transformed from an age-old handi-craft to semiskilled labor. Just as these printers attained mastery of their craft, computer technology made hands-on application of their mastery superfluous.

Some, as we have seen, were excited by the challenge of re-training. But for others, the honeymoon was shortlived. Recall the complaints of keyboard operators in previous chapters—work-ing with cold-type pasteup, former hot-metal printers use words like "soul-destroying," "there's nothing to it," "there's no challenge anymore," to describe the new processes.

At the *New York Times,* where the majority of the paper's printers were retrained, automation is reported to have drastically diminished the workload, destroying much of the pleasure and meaning of work in the composing room. In Rogers and Fried-man's *Printers Face Automation,* printers at the *Times* describe the composing room: "Boredom is a big problem," "The glamour is gone," "It's miserable."[43]

In sum, the printers' story is a story of decline: the discontin-uity in occupational identity, the loss of the craftspeople's control and the commensurate status, the disruption in the anticipated occupational cycle of novitiate, apprentice, journeyman, and mas-ter printer. A generation of printers has missed its turn at selec-tion; unable to teach, unable to pass on quality, these printers are cheated out of posterity. The union hall becomes a sad place. And then it ceases to exist. These men and women are losing just when they should be gaining esteem.

It is here that we can speculate on the function of occupational narrative and active nostalgia—that which inspires a rhetoric of tradition. In examining the actuality of the old days, it is a wonder that such a noisy, dirty, demanding, and dangerous world not only became a source of nostalgic reminiscence and pride, but that it is used as evidence of the superiority of times past. Feeling nostalgic is not simply remembering and recalling the past, it is imbuing the past with special qualities. This reconstructive whitewash of, and yearning for, the past is the essence of nostalgia.

Deriving from the Greek root *nostros* ("return home") and *algos* ("pain"), nostalgia originally meant aggravated homesickness or painful yearning for some past period or irrecoverable condition. In time the word has lost its pathological connotations and become the noun used to describe a sentimental "feeling"—a positive longing for the past, for which no antonym exists. Nostalgia is basically a cultural repository. It conserves.[44]

Sociologist Fred Davis hypothesizes that discontinuity in life experience fosters nostalgia. In his book *Yearning for Yesterday: A Sociology of Nostalgia,* Davis shows how nostalgia serves to recover a sense of identity in a time marked by major change. "Nostalgia is most pronounced at transitional phases in the life cycle that call for identity change and adaptation. . . ."[45] In short, nostalgia assuages threats to identity continuity engendered by problematic life transitions. It is *how* printers contrast their former world of work with the present that constitutes nostalgia. By muting the negative, they soften the blow to their occupational identity wrought by the change to cold type. The rhetoric of nostalgia allows them to link an imagined former better time, in which they thought well of themselves, with an uncertain and unforgiving present.

It is through the rhetoric of endangered tradition that the printers' lost esteem is redeemed. The "then" of a legendary past restores dignity through talk of a time when printers wore high hats. The "what happened" of changing talk explains the transformation that has taken place. And the comparison of "then" to "now" in adaptation talk reestablishes the printers' concept of themselves as craftspeople above other labor crafts. Through narrative, they associate themselves with a past which symbolizes a time when they felt they could control type. The world of hot metal, depicted in occupational nostalgia, exists in retrospect as compensation for losses suffered.

In Search of Metaphors

In a 1931 American Historical Association presidential address, Carl Becker attempted to identify the essential nature and function of his discipline. "Let us admit that there are two histories: the actual series of events that once occurred; and the ideal series that we affirm and hold in memory." The latter, Becker suggested, is a mythological adaptation of the former, an imaginative, useful creation, which "everyman" fashions out of social memory and his own individual experience.[46]

This book is built upon the wisdom of everyman historians. Were they asked, these printers might also distinguish and admit to two histories, one being the actual series of events that have occurred in printing technology, and the other being their nostalgia, a mythological adaptation to what actually happened. The latter is like an echo on the former, reverberating off the hard, cold walls of the absolute.

What is significant about this microcosm of technological unemployment and human adaptation? It is significant that people make peace with lost status and the deskilling of craft labor through the voicing of patterned expressive forms. The printers' experience confirms the vitality of occupational folklore and group identity, despite dispersements in space and despair in spirits. Their collective experience teaches us that the nostalgic impulse is at once intimately private and unmistakably social. In this instance, it finds expression in the rhetoric of tradition, a lesson forged by generations of hot-metal printers. Once voiced, one finds surprising consistency in the themes, narrative forms, and functions of nostalgia.

In the making and maintaining of occupational group identity, these men and women have sustained a sense of meaningful connection and continuity, in the face of unwelcome change. Such mythological adaptations, in an age of an ever-increasing supply of technological retirees, is a creative social act worthy of our attention.

When Ed Jacob sought to identify himself with a particular breed of craftsmen, he conjured up the picture of a dead printer. The ink-stained corpse serves as a fitting metaphor for the death of printing craftsmanship. We must leave it to the next generation to supply us with new metaphors.

Notes

1. Cf. Briggs's discussion of rhetorical competence valued by the Mexicanos of northern New Mexico. The spoken and musical folklore of this community is referred to collectively as "the talk of the elders of bygone days." Briggs reports that the present elders view the transmission of this "talk" as crucial to the survival of Mexicano culture. Briggs, *Learning How to Ask,* 37.

2. *The Printer* 11 (November 1986): 4.

3. Typesetting a book costs a certain amount of money (what is called a "plant cost" in the trade) and it varies inversely with the number of copies printed. If the typesetting costs $6,000 and one prints 1,000 copies, then the typesetting cost is $6.00 per unit. Print 10,000 copies and the typesetting cost drops to 60 cents. If 100,000 copies are printed, the typesetting cost crops to 6 cents.

4. The poor copying of the *Garamond* typeface, as shown in the phototypeset Knopf example, also demonstrates how phototype distorts and degrades the beauty of the original typeface's hot-metal letters.

5. Moxon, *Mechanick Exercises,* 217.

6. Dell Hymes, "Folklore's Nature and the Sun's Myth," *Journal of American Folklore* 88 (1975): 351.

7. See Robert S. McCarl, "Occupational Folklife: A Theoretical Hypothesis," in *Working Americans: Contemporary Approaches to Occupational Folklife* (Washington, D.C.: Smithsonian Institution, 1978).

8. Interview with Bertram A. Powers at No. 6 headquarters in lower Manhattan, 1 November 1985.

9. Carl Schlesinger, personal communication, February 1990.

10. Archie Green wrote this story from memory on 19 July 1987, having carried it in his head since 1941.

11. Barbara Babcock defines narrative metacommunication as "any element of communication which calls attention to the speech event as a performance and the relationship which obtains between the narrator and his audience vis-a-vis the narrative message." In other words, metacommunication is any framing device which both categorizes and comments upon the communication taking place. It is as if the speaker were momentarily stepping outside of the narrative mode in order to grab the listener's attention. See Babcock, "The Story in the Story: Metanarration in Folk Narrative," in Richard Bauman, *Verbal Art as Performance* (Prospect Heights, Ill.: Waveland Press, 1984), 66.

12. Dick Harrison, tape-recorded interview in his office, 23 November 1983. Emphasis added.

13. Ed Jacob, tape-recorded interview during lunch, 30 November 1983.

14. Ibid.

15. Tape-recorded interview at Heritage Printers in Charlotte, North Carolina, 13 November 1986.

16. Amelia Story, tape-recorded interview in her room at the Union Printers Home, 3 February 1988.

17. Tape-recorded interview at Heritage Printers, 13 November 1986.

18. John Peckham, emeritus employee at Meriden-Stinehour Press, interview, 21 February 1986.

19. Carl Gross, told to me during work, 2 November 1983.

20. Ed Jacob, tape-recorded interview, 30 November 1983.

21. Bob Culp, tape-recorded lunch conversation at Kelly and Cohen's, Philadelphia, 14 March 1986.

22. Rick Newell, tape-recorded interview at Heritage Printers, 14 November 1986.

23. Dick Harrison, interview, 24 October 1983.

24. F. J. Hurlbut, "Decline of the Book Printer," *Inland Printer,* June 1890, from Annenberg, *Typographic Journey,* 331.

25. In the musical system of solmization, sol-fa syllables are used to designate notes in a scale. In the "fixed do" system syllables are applied to notes of the C major scale (i.e., C = do, D = re, etc.) and remain fixed regardless of key. In the "movable do" system, "do" is assigned to the tonic and will designate a different note depending on the key in which one is singing.

26. Williams, *The Country and the City,* 21.

27. Tape-recorded interview at Heritage Printers, 13 November 1986. Earl Powell's story of the comparatively long hours worked in the past is typical of

the occupational narratives spoken by older workers. One of the retired fishermen in Lloyd and Mullen's book tells a similar story of bravado. ". . . Well God, I've got the record where I can show you where I would work from Labor Day to Thanksgiving and not have a day off, which was seven days a week when you was fishing. . . . That's the way you worked then, you know. If you were fishing, you had to make it while the fish were around. We didn't take any days off. We was there." Alva Snell quoted in Lloyd and Mullen, *Lake Erie Fishermen,* 87–88.

28. The idea of social distancing comes from the teachings of Ray Birdwhistell. Social distance is gained in a variety of ways. He tells the following story: "In 'I Remember Mama' they used a Swedish immigrant lady. This was in the midwest where she had an accent. They could take up topics that are now only appearing in afternoon soap operas." Personal communication, February 1985.

29. Tape-recorded interview with Dan Burns at his home, 13 September 1985.

30. Ed Jacob, tape-recorded interview at Datacomp, 30 November 1983.

31. Tape-recorded lunch conversation with Bob Culp at Kelly and Cohen's, Philadelphia, 14 March 1986.

32. Charles Miner, conversation at Union Printers Home, 3 February 1988.

33. Carl Gross, communication during work, 2 November 1983.

34. Fil Valdez, tape-recorded interview, 2 February 1988.

35. Quoted in Rogers and Friedman, *Printers Face Automation,* 121.

36. Cockburn, *Brothers,* 107–8.

37. Conversation in John Peckham's office at Meriden-Stinehour Press, Meriden, Connecticut, 21 February 1986.

A Long Island bayman in Peter Mathiessen's *Men's Lives: The Surfmen and Baymen of the South Fork* (New York: Random House, 1986) tells a similar then/now narrative. As in Earl Powell's overtime story, he recites tall-tale figures, and as in John Peckham's story, he criticizes the apparent weakness of workers today. "Course everything changes, y'know. Was thinkin just the other day about chunks. A chunk was a heavy box, loaded around 350 pounds. Back before we used sugar boxes, carry five-six hundred pounds, used to cart 'em around by hand, and the railroad men, too. Men these days gettin awful weak, seems like, because the boxes are gettin smaller all the time. After the chunks we had them shad boxes, with partitions, carried maybe 280; then there was a 200-pound box; then the 125-pound crate that we used in them years you [Mathiessen] was fishin with us. Now the wood boxes are all gone, they use them cardboard cartons, hold about 60–70 pounds apiece" (page 43). "The guys today have it darn easy; they don't work now like my father worked, they ride around . . ." (143).

38. Halper, *The Foundry,* 77.

39. Ed Jacob, tape-recorded interview at Datacomp, 30 November 1983.

40. Bill Loftin, tape recorded in his office at Heritage Printers, 13 November 1986.

41. Powers made these comments upon retiring from his post of twenty-nine years as Local 6 president. The conversational context was his assessment of the Reagan administration's success in union busting during the air-traffic controllers' strike. See David E. Pitt, "His Vision Realized, a Union Leader Retires," *New York Times,* 15 June 1990.

42. Earl Powell, tape-recorded in Bill Loftin's office at Heritage Printers, 13 November 1986.

43. Rogers and Friedman, *Printers Face Automation,* 121. These descriptions of the composing room were made in 1979, just after the *New York Times* got rid of their Linotype machines and made the changeover to automated photo-electronic printing.

44. Fred Davis, *Yearning for Yesterday: A Sociology of Nostalgia* (New York: Free Press, 1979); see his chapter on nostalgia and the life cycle, 52–71.

45. Ibid., 49.

46. Carl Becker, *Everyman His Own Historian: Essays on History and Politics;* (1935 reprint; New York: Quadrangle Books, 1966), 234 and 245.

Index

Accidents, 51–52
Allen, Greer, 119–20, 135–36
Aller, Paul, 192
Allied Printing Trade Association, 7
Anderson, Sherwood, xv, 171
Anthropomorphism: of computer equipment, 158; of letterpress printing, 120; in printing terminology, 78; of type, 75, 134–35
Apprenticeship: decrease in training, 171–73; demise of, 165, 173; guidance from journeymen printers, 28, 169, 174–75; in hot-metal composition, xiv, 1, 26–27; initiatory rituals, 63, 69–72; length of, 88; mid-twentieth-century, 143; socialization during, 63, 169, 177–78; training during, 169, 172–75; union control over, 132
Aristocracy of labor, 165
Auction, 139–42
Automation: of composition process, 119; ITU response to, 28, 131–32; and skilled jobs, 179n.13

Bacon, Francis, xv
Barnett, George, 118
Becker, Carl, 216
Benzine, 52, 69
Bevis, Sandy, 6–7
Big Six. See New York Typographical Union
Birdwhistell, Ray, 11

Blauner, Robert, 18
Breckman, Irv, 198
Bridges, Harry, 31
Brotherhood, among printers, 166, 196
Burns, Dan, 123, 148, 166–67, 181, 184–85, 186, 204–5; mentioned, 57, 91, 165
Byrne, Allen, 165

Caldwell, Erskine, xv, 171
Campbell, Bob, 27–28, 91, 175
Chairman of chapel. See Chapel: role of chairman
Chamberlain, Ollie, 82
Chapel: ancient customs of 57–60, 62–63; role of chairman, 57 58
Childs, George, 34
Chilton Publishing, 27, 53, 57, 91
Clemens, Samuel, 171. See also Twain, Mark
Commons, John, 169
Communications Workers of America, 22n.13, 24n.30, 45
Composing stick, 87, 95n.71, 193
Compositor (sculpture), 12, 13
Compositors: defined, 6–7; newspaper, 80, status of, xiv; versus pressmen, 6. See also Printers; Hand composition
Computer-aided typesetting: advent of, 3; generations of, 129, 136; and job security, 158–59; at Packard Press, 155; quality of, 138–39; speed of, 136–38. See also Photocomposition;

A Note on the Author

Maggie Holtzberg-Call holds a Ph.D. in folklore from the University of Pennsylvania. As an independent researcher she has been affiliated with the Alabama State Council on the Arts and the Georgia Folklife Program. Dr. Holtzberg-Call has published articles about black railroad crews in the South and about printing and the rhetoric of tradition. She is currently producing a film on gandy dancers.

Books in the Series Folklore and Society

George Magoon and the Down East Game War:
History, Folklore, and the Law
Edward D. Ives

Diversities of Gifts: Field Studies
in Southern Religion
Edited by Ruel W. Tyson, Jr., James L. Peacock, and
Daniel W. Patterson

Days from a Dream Almanac
Dennis Tedlock

Nowhere in America:
The Big Rock Candy Mountain and Other Comic Utopias
Hal Rammel

The Lost World of the Craft Printer
Maggie Holtzberg-Call

Listening to Old Voices: Folklore
in the Lives of Nine Elderly People
Patrick B. Mullen